BRIDGE

Spring/Summer 2002

Volume 1, (Love Will Not Be Mocked) Number 4

All contents © 2002 Bridge Magazine

Founded: Anno Domini MM
ISSN #: 1531-4766
ISBN #: 0-9705782-3-7

Michael Workman, Publisher & Editor-In-Chief
Mark Tschaepe, Culture & Critique Editor-At-Large
Greg Purcell, Poetry Editor
Marie Walz, Designer & Art Editor
Howard Fonda, Associate Editor, Art
David Andrews, Associate Editor, Literature
Project Pages Guest Curators: Iain Muirhead & Amavong Panya, NFA Space

Readers: David Andrews, Chris Andrews, Marie Walz, Greg Gillam, Valerie Palmer, Jake Juros, Greg Purcell, Mike Newirth, Ralph Syverson, Jay Niimi, David David Katzman, Jennifer Kubik

Our fine print this issue, sadly, is committed, in part, to addressing Things We Said We'd Do But Haven't. First off, regular readers will notice a missing letters section. Besides not receiving any mail in our box, we had too much other good stuff to print. Ergo, no letters, no section. A casualty of our willingness to allow an experiment to fail if not adequate to its intended purposes. Similarly, our promised "Poor Charlie" timeline also fails to appear, for which we do not apologize. In all honesty, none of us are sure what to do with "Poor Charlie," and, not necessarily an unfortunate circumstance in our opinion, his timeline may never be published.

Onto brighter concerns: thanks this issue go out to Ideotech/Open End Art for their large-format printing services and for hosting this issue's release party; to Ralph Syverson and Yuki Kokubo for *again* lending their loft for our slush brunch, and special props go to Ralph for donating his Mac memory card and for stepping in last minute to help us with image-scanning difficulties. Thanks also need to go out to Tony Wight at Bodybuilder & Sportsman Gallery for making our interview with Jeanne Dunning possible; Angela Weaser at Dalkey Archive Press for her help with RCF and Sorrentino images; Meredith Goldsmith for her valiant advertising volunteerism and stick-to-itiveness.

Thanks in advance also go to everybody helping to make our late-April/early-May spring tour—with stops in Chicago, Spokane and Seattle, Washington, Portland, Oregon, Los Angeles, California and New York City—a success.

Make sure to have a peek at our website (www.bridgemagazine.org), newly and brilliantly redesigned by *Bridge* Art Editor & Designer, Marie Walz. Improvements include a function for purchasing back issues and subscribing online; more specific spring tour information, including locations and times for readings/events (including where you'll be able to find us at BookExpo, Art Chicago, and Printer's Row Book Fair) is also available.

BRIDGE IS DISTRIBUTED BY THE FOLLOWING COMPANIES:

Canada
Marginal Distribution
277 George Street North,
Unit 102
Peterborough, Ontario
Canada K9J 3G9
Ph: (705) 745-2326
Fax: (705) 745-2122
marginal@ptbo.igs.net
www.marginalbook.com

U.S.
Bernhard DeBoer
113 East Centre Street
Nutley, NJ 07110
Ph: (973) 667-9300
Fax: (973) 667-0086

Ingram Book Group
One Ingram Blvd.
P.O. Box 3006
La Vergne, TN 37086-1986
Ph: (800) 937-8000
Fax: (800) 876-0186
www.ingrambookgroup.com

Last Gasp
777 Florida Street
San Francisco, CA 94103
415-241-2420
www.lastgasp.com

Media Solutions
c/o Keith Jacobs
1217 Heil Quaker Blvd.
LaVergne, TN 37086
Ph: (615) 213-0081

Tower Records
Check local listings for info

France
Dif'Pop*
Ph: 33 1 40 24 21 31

U.K.
Central Books*
99 Wallis Road
London, England
E9 5LN
Ph: +44 208 986 4854

Portugal
Assirio & Alvim*
c/o Lucia Pinho e Melo
Rua Sao Nicolau
119 1st Floor
1100/548 Lisboa
Ph: 351 21 324 0640

* *Still waiting for final cofirmati*

For a complete list, please visit our website (address below).

SUBSCRIPTIONS: INDIVIDUALS: $17.00; FOREIGN, ADD $3.50. INSTITUTIONS: $26.00; FOREIGN, ADD $3.50.

Bridge is published triannually-ish by *Bridge Inc.*, is almost a not-for-profit corporation (please check our website for official announcements of our application status). Donations will be tax-deductible to the extent allowed by the law. The editors of *Bridge* welcome submissions of essays, fiction, poetry and art. All submissions must be accompanied by an SASE. For our editorial interests, please see the submission link on our website at **www.bridgemagazine.org** (but be forewarned — our guidelines describe a structure present everywhere and nowhere here). Please send address changes and all other correspondence to us at **1357 North Ashland Avenue, #3A Chicago, IL 60622**. Email: **submissions**

BRIDGE

CONTENTS

READINGS

Brian Costello 2 *Hayseed Out of Unincorporated Seminole County*
CJ Mitchell 3 *Walking in Chicago*
BC Brown 8 *The Face of Love*
Kevin Sampsell 9 *Blowjob*

FICTION

Joe Meno 21 *Mr. Song*
Caitlin O'Connor Creevy 35 *Girl Games*
Ryan Kenealy 67 *The Pot Roast Consultant*
Curtis White 78 *Your Aunt Is Dead*
Harvey Strub 82 *Three Letters To the President*

INTERVIEWS

Michael Workman 13 *Alex Shakar*
Meredith Goldsmith 102 *Jeanne Dunning*

CULTURE & CRITIQUE

Kevin Blasko 110 *Art After Humanity*
Jan Estep 118 *A State of Hypoxia*
Mark Tschaepe 125 *Pheno-meme-ology of the Cellph: An analy-sis of evolution through the habitual use of a technological appendage*
Michelle Grabner & Brad Killam 131 *Ideal Avalanche*

Bridge *Critical Portfolio: Gilbert Sorrentino & The Review of Contemporary Fiction:* 136

David Andrews 138 *"Something Has Sure As Hell Happened": Gilbert Sorrentino,* The Review of Contemporary Fiction, *and Provocative Fiction*

Robert McLaughlin **144** *Sorrentino Bookends:* The Review of Contemporary Fiction, *the Academy, and Literary Culture*
Nicholas Mosley **149** *The Review of Contemporary Fiction*
Jerome Klinkowitz **152** *Career Moves*
Toby Olson **157** *Sorrentino's Opus*
159 *Works By Gilbert Sorrentino*
David Andrews **160** *Ever the Consummate, Intransigent Modernist*

POETRY

DA Powell **20** *Looking For Mr. G. Bar*
Joyelle McSweeney, Three Poems:
27 *The Premier*
28 *Interview With A Dog*
30 *Joy*
Peter Richards, Three Poems:
52 *Pastoral*
53 *Waiting For You*
54 *Thursday With Gelatinous Shawl*
Joel Craig, Three Poems:
64 *The Tree of Life (After Chagall)*
65 *On the Orphan's Tongue*

PROJECT PAGES & ART

Gean Moreno & William Cordova **91**

ILLUSTRATIONS, INCIDENTAL ART, DOODLES, SKETCHES, DRAWINGS

Shana Lutker
Ralph Syverson
Michael Jefferson
Howard Fonda

Cover by Michael Jefferson
P-Head Trading Cards by Patrick W. Welch
Co-Designed by Dan Raeburn

This issue was designed in part while listening to The Magnetic Fields CD collection, 69 Love Songs

Letter From the Editor

Michael Workman

In "Future," a brief look at "a premise for a society of the future" in his collection, *Roadside Dog*, poet Czeslaw Milosz speculates that "poetry survives amid the generalized savagery, now health in the midst of sickness, just as once it was sickness in the midst of health." I've consistently been struck by the response of some who have never read *Bridge* when I describe our interest in publishing literature, visual arts, culture and critique. Invariably the reaction I witness is a supercilious disbelief in the viability of combining these practices and a circumspect approach to creative imagination no less fixed than if an armed burglar were bagging the family silver in the next room. I suspect that such reticence is largely due to having themselves done the bagging, and a subsequent fatalism that looks to pessimism and an eager pathology for explanation—at the expense of all amelioration. Pitiful—and typical of the obstacles not only to our little publishing concern, but to a healthy society.

Appropriately then, starting from the end of this issue, we take a look at a few other publications—one prosperous, one gone forever—who have fought to preserve inspiration amidst the generalized savagery. While not a complete picture of innovators whose efforts flow in *Bridge's* veins, to us both are important predecessors. Associate Editor Dave Andrews convenes a belated 20th-anniversary look back at the inaugural issue of *The Review of Contemporary Fiction* and the to-date lifework of Dalkey Archive Press author Gilbert Sorrentino, while Michelle Grabner and Brad Killam offer a retrospective on the extinct 1960's New York publication, *Avalanche*.

I'm pleased we can offer some inspiration of our own, this issue showcasing new fiction by Ryan Kenealy, Joe Meno, Elizabeth Crane, Caitlin O'Connor Creevy, and new poetry by Peter Richards, Joyelle McSweeney, D.A. Powell and Joel Craig. In interview, *Savage Girl* author Alex Shakar craftily lambastes American marketing and our American market culture, while artist Jeanne Dunning discusses her Blobs, Puddles and Tom Thumb with Meredith Goldsmith. Following the "Evolution and Technology" theme of our Culture & Critique section this issue, *New Art Examiner* Editor Jan Estep explores hypoxia—a deficiency in the amount of oxygen reaching bodily tissue at high altitudes—as a metaphor for the quest for knowledge. C&C Editor-at-Large M.D. Tschaepe muses on the role of cell phones in modern life, combining technology with the concept of the self to reflect drolly on the "cellph." Also this issue, we debut the first in a multi-part series of trading cards created by Patrick W. Welch and co-designed by *The Imp* Editor Dan Raeburn. Ten in all, with the complete package available through our website, www.bridgemagazine.org.

A final note of encouragement: if you have yet to subscribe to *Bridge*, soon to be a full-fledged not-for-profit publication, don't delay. Complete and mail back the enclosed dinky little suscription envelope today. Besides saving a few sawbucks, if you're reading this, then you too have a stake in what we do—and can help us do it better. You can also support our advertising efforts by filling out and mailing in the Reader Survey at the back of this issue. Thanks for your help.

~BRIDGE READINGS~

HAYSEED OUT OF UNINCORPORATED SEMINOLE COUNTY FLORIDA

Brian Costello

(*Author Note*: Any similarities between the following memoir and Dorothy Allison's *Bastard Out of Carolina* are not purely coincidental. Thank you.)

Ah wuz ihn thuh sevinth grayed whin Ah wuz xpelld frum skew-ell fer spontemporanusly combustin' tayin see guls weeth Alkee Seltzur durin mah luhnsh brake. Ah wuzint skeered Ah coulda dun gawn bayk buht taint ihn mah naychur tuh dew soh. Ahm frum uhninkor-prayted sayminol cowntee ihn sintril floorduhh an yew lissen them fam-lees livin theyur theyull teyull yew them Costello klayun aint nuthin buht uh macin jur uh bayud bidness.

Noh Costello nevir mayd et passd thuh sevinth grayde naught mah Unkuls Jim Jem, Zachary Zed, Billy Boo, Durfee Dean, Kenny Clyde, naught mah Aints Maddie Loo, Shaley Shoo, Wynona Wee, Ashley Day, Tanya Troo, surtinlee naught mah cuzins Suzie Q, Sheila E, Skeeter, Skeeter Sr the 3rd, Stevie Bee, TJ, AJ, BJ, Honey Pie, Belinda Mae, Patsy Poo, Becky Lynn, Wanda Rae, Janet Jae, Markee Moo, Sammy Strom an naught evin Duke an Ah wuz jussd lahk theyum.

Looken bayuck Ah woodin bee fexin tuh chayng nuthin cuz thayut wuz thuh bayust twunny dollersh Ah ayver mayde whin Ah beyut Brayndun Meelee thayut see guls buloh uhp eef yew fee-dum Alkee Seltzur.

Whee wur setin owtsahd ayut th eyun uv th lowung ros uv woodin tabels me en mah gurlfraynd Mary Kay en Brayndun an heeyus gurlfraynd Sally May an wee wur watchen ahl thuh see gulz swoopen an poopen roun evree budees maters an taters. Brayndun hee startid uhp gen sayin

"Brahn, yer dummer then uh mewul stuk en uh jahr uh moonshahn. Alkee Seltzurs don bulow uhp no see gulz."

"Ah reckin thay due an Ahl bayut yew twehntee dahlerz sez thay due uh huh."

"Fahn," Brayndun sayud, spittin own hes hayund caykd weeth durt frum pecken hominee en thuh feelds ahl dey. "Shayke awn et."

Ah sheeook awn et an nex dey, Ah stole Mommuh Mollee Hatchits bocks uh Alkee Seltzurs frum owur owthows medysin cabbynit. Whee ayte luyunch thuh nex dey an Ah tuk owt mah bocks uh Alkee Seltzers frum th frun pokit uh mah over hauls raht nex tuh mah cayun uh copinhagin an teeyupeetowd uhp tew uh flok uh see gulz hoo wur etin rounuh garbije cayun. Ah tossd theyum Alkee Selzurs lak an ol mayun fedin duks en thuh parrk lahk uh yankey tuh shamd be farten en puhblik. Nex theeng Ah no theyum see gulz paykd thuh Alkee Seltzur weeyuth thayur beeks ahl teyun uh theyum an theyun thay fuhlew uhway.

Furst nuthin hapind et wuz sahlint thayun BOOM! Thuh furst wun buhlew uhp twentee fit ehn thuh ayur theyun thuh secin wun BOOM fallen lahk shaht dayewn eyeraki playns.

"Sunufabeetch!" Brayndon yayeld.

"Whoooo-hooo!" Ah yayeld.

Thayun uh wissle frum th princy-pulls mowth hoo keekd mee owt an mah Daddee Gasper Goo gaht mee en hes truhk an sed

"Brahn yew uh Costello an thayut meenz yew lak uh heyun howz en a shayurcroperz turnihp jahr."

Ah don claym tuh bee noh colij bohy buht ayt leest Ah dew no thayut see gulz bulow uhp whin yew feehdum Alkee Seltzur soh thayur thee eyund.

WALKING IN CHICAGO

CJ Mitchell

How did you start?

Saturday April 8, 2000, 8.30am. Almost at the city's edge, we start our walk south. Columbia 6750N. Within five minutes we have walked on side-walk, sand, ice, salt, grass. The tideline of Lake Michigan is high – we walk along the beach from Columbia to North Shore, then cut in west to Sheridan, resuming our walk south. The sun is sharp, the cold piercing. We walk under the train line at Loyola – the station I enter and exit eight or more times each week, going to or coming home from work. We need to get indoors. I should have brought a hat.

What did you eat and drink?

Viva Java café, Granville 6200N: faces tingling from the cold as soon as we enter. Coffee and croissants. Bob Marley CD playing.

10.10am Kopi café – a traveller's café, on Clark 5400N, Andersonville – earl grey tea; granola, yoghurt, dried fruit – indian tea: oatmeal and milk, fruit – 10 year old girl at nearby table reading a book about NYC – a voice from another table announces, "I'm pro-choice, I've never supported pro-life legislation." Karen feeling wind burns, not prepared for this unexpected wind, legs cold, lip balm.

10.50, called Sarah regarding our plan to meet with her at 2pm.

Change tray has diagram map of the London Underground system.

Uncommon Ground: espresso/tea: Grace 3800N.

Belmont 12.35pm 3200N: Moti Mahal – buffet lunch of Indian food: samosas, vegetable curry, rice, nan bread, and water.

3pm, Karen has tea from Coffee and Tea exchange on Armitage 2000N.

What were the colors of the blossoms?

A canopy of blossoms looking east, stretching over the street. Cutting east off Broadway onto Berwyn, 5300N. Off the main street, the colors of blossoms: white, pink, purple, blue. Ceud Mille Faite – a gaelic greeting painted above a doorway. Ice falling off trees and lampposts – melted ice draining down the sides of buildings.

Approaching Belmont, 12.30pm: red tulips. Ice steadily melting in drips off telegraph wires.

Walking east on North 1600N, 4pm. Clear blue sky. Neighborhood Commons Cooperative, on the edge of Cabrini Green, in Old Town, the edge of old and new buildings. The blooms: white and purple. Magnolias everywhere. Turning south onto LaSalle, groomed bushes and young trees line the streets.

Who was with you?

My wife, Karen Christopher. She divides her breakfast insulin shots into two parts: the first at the Viva Java café, the second at the Kopi café in Andersonville. Karen calls her friend Liz from a public phone at Ardmore 5800N, while I peer into storefronts. We're wondering if there's a chance of meeting with Liz later on the walk, but get her answerphone. Karen calls again around lunchtime, and again gets the answerphone – Liz later receives these updates of our progress south, too late to join us.

Walking south on Broadway to Briar Street, to meet with Sarah. Karen has an insulin reaction at 1.50pm, and we sit on a wooden bench on Briar, sunlight dazzling. We're outside Sarah's apartment block: 540 West Briar, Vintage Charm - studios, one bedroom, two bedrooms. Wexenthaller Realty Management Office. A converted hotel: what is the history of this building? It reminds us of the Hotel in The Shining.

Sarah is walking with us to the 1926 Exhibition Studies Space on Halsted – carrying food and drink which she's bought and prepared for the free dinners which are being distributed at 1926 during the Counter Productive Industries project. We walk south on Halsted, past the Fullerton/Lincoln junction at DePaul University. A slow and steady hour, talking with Sarah.

Why did you do this?

The walk was a response of sorts to Iain Sinclair's book *Lights out for the Territory* – a series of essays recording walks in London undertaken by Sinclair and his companion, photographer Marc Atkins. The first essay, "Skating on Thin Eyes – The First Walk" begins:

"The notion was to cut a crude V into the sprawl of the city, to vandalise dormant energies by an act of ambulant signmaking. To walk out from Hackney to Greenwich Hill, and back along the River Lea to Chingford Mount, recording and retrieving the messages on walls, lampposts, doorjambs: the spites and spasms of an increasingly deranged populace. (I had developed this curious conceit while working on my novel *Radon Daughters*: that the physical movements of the characters across their territory might spell out the letters of a secret alphabet. Dynamic shapes, with ambitions to achieve a life of their own, quite independent of their supposed author. Railway to pub to hospital: trace the line on the map. These botched runes, burnt into the script in the heat of creation, offer an alternative reading – a subterranean, preconscious text capable of divination and prophecy. A sorcerer's grimoire that would function as a curse or a blessing.)"

Sinclair is interested in the unseen, forgotten and hidden, along with what is revealed on the surface, and how these all relate to each other. His knowledge of contemporary culture and his immersion in arcane and occult history is extensive: locations described resonate with energies from decades if not centuries earlier.

I remembered Bruce Chatwin's *The Songlines*, a partly-fictional account of Chatwin's travels in Australia, and his research into Aboriginal songlines. The book culminates with a deeply moving thesis that human beings are essentially nomadic, we live through walking, and our walking can chart song maps which tell of the routes we have taken. I also recalled Paul Auster's *New York Trilogy*, which includes one character secretly following another, whose walks through NYC seem aimless and without purpose. It becomes apparent in time that each walk forms (from a bird's eye view, looking down on the city) a massive letter – and after a number of days those letters spell the words TOWER OF BABEL. The city becomes a search for language, writing on its surface through walking.

This walk would be through a city I am only beginning to know, to link locations I've experienced discretely, after arriving by car, bus or train. It would also serve as a physical connection between home and work – my commute south, walking south, weaving approximately around the route of the CTA Red Line, taking as long as required. This commute would extend to the length of a working day. There was no specific agenda to the walk, only to walk, observe, connect.

How can 13 miles be described?

Cutting a line from north to south. Slicing through the thoroughfare. A red line, a life lined vein or artery, flowing from home to work. Mimicking the train line, we follow the route I travel to work, from Rogers Park to downtown – only by foot. Thirteen miles has a duration of eight and a half hours.

Granville 6200N – Popeyes/Dunkin Donuts: we could be anywhere. A thin layer of skin is eroded, the sole of my shoes diminish. The particles distributed along the route, blown into doorways.

What rested on the surface?

6700N: God Bless: written in pink felt tip pen on white paper – a Fannie May wrapper – Traffic light fixture lying on the sidewalk – an Earpiece from Walkman headphones – Damp, crumpled newspaper . . . 6200N: Footprints in concrete sidewalk . . . Hollywood 5700N: Shell/Amoco stations, servicing the link to Lake Shore Drive. Broken green glass – Marlboro cigarette packet . . . 4900N: St Boniface Cemetery, cracks in the tarmac – "let perpetual light shone upon them, poor handmaids of Jesus Christ" followed by 19 names – the sound of jets in the sky . . . 4800N Lawrence: walking from Clark to Broadway, the tarmac on the street has strangely worked its way up over edge of the sidewalk. Karen says it looks like a "slow bruise" . . . East to Clark on Montrose 4400N: leaf imprints in the concrete, detailed veins on leaves . . . The sole of my feet pressed down. The body weight, the body frame pressed down.

What was written on the surface?

Yellow and pink writing: planned cuts in tar, concrete. We encounter aerosol can writing on the sidewalks and roads: numbers, lines, arrows – officially sanctioned graffiti, proposing future repairs or improvements to gas, electricity, cable, water supplies. Hidden layers of utilities, systems unknown to us. Each surface is provisional – waiting for another layer to be added. The tarmac has strangely worked its way up over edge of the sidewalk. Karen says it looks like a "slow bruise."

Where was the ice?

Ice on the sides of trees, public phones, postboxes, steps; patches on the sidewalk.

New condo block, 50% sold, drainpipes not yet attached – melted ice draining down sides of the building and pooling at base. Across the street, Quality Excavation Inc are demolishing 3232 Seminary.

Just over the River, warning signs are out for Falling Ice – as we cross the bridge, we see ice chunks gracefully falling downwards to the sidewalk.

What do you remember?

A childhood friend often walked in the gutters, dragging his heels, finding treasures: one time, a 5 pound note. Another day, with snow and slush on the streets, I trudged back and forwards through the gutters, enjoying the movements of wet slush around my boots – my ten minute walk home at lunchtime from school extended to 30 minutes or more, before my mother came out to find me still over a block away from home where food was waiting for me.

Tell us about the event you attended.

3pm at the 1926 Exhibition Studies Space on Halsted. A discussion event: Renegotiating the Public Sphere, part of the Counter Productive Industries project. Greg Sholette talks about the use of street space, anti-gentrification, acting locally/thinking globally. Greg is involved with the collective REPOhistory in NYC, whose recent project Circulation includes charting red and blue lines through that city: blood consignment routes. A quote from the Critical Art Ensemble: public space is only public to a certain degree, then the cracks show.

How did your knees feel?

My left knee began to get sore just before lunchtime – on the outside of the knee. I used to hike regularly, as a teenager, with the Scouts or with friends, but not much recently. My father walked the West Highland Way in the early 90s, he was around 60 at the time. A six day walk from Fort William to Glasgow, I met him at the conclusion of the walk and we went out for a meal. I had imagined him limping, a creeping walk, affected in some way from his long route, but he seemed fine, full of energy, not even particularly tired. My knees grew increasingly sore as the afternoon wore on, on the outside of both knees. Going up and down steps, edges of sidewalk particularly hurt. My walking speed was greatly reduced by late afternoon, and for two days afterwards, stairs were difficult.

What did you think about?

We could be anywhere . . . Broadway and Belmont, 3300N: the satisfaction of seeing a street curve out of sight within three blocks, not constrained by the rigid grid system, but echoing the coastline . . . a countdown from 6750N to ZERO . . . a church spire surrounded by high rise blocks, far outshadowed by modern housing and commercial needs . . . he walked everywhere in Chicago . . . Idea for performance: memorize the streets names from home to work . . . Kevin Newhall's recent project for Counter Productive Industries: on his commute from Edgewater to Downtown, getting the bus passengers to applaud every time a new person came on board; and then waving goodbye whenever anyone left the bus.

What did you hear?

Bob Marley in the Viva Java cafe; Drum practice from a second floor room on the west side of Broadway, 5800N; Lou Reed in the Kopi café (am I more conscious of sound in interior, enclosed spaces?); jets in the sky above St. Boniface Cemetary; water draining down the sides of buildings; Bob Marley, a muffled soundtrack from inside a house, just off Belmont; through the subway grills on State Street, the rumble of trains underneath your feet; a religious preacher talking loudly at the corner of State and Washington; train lines overhead on Wabash, trains drowning our conversation.

How did you finish?

At 4:30pm, we visit the Zolla Lieberman Gallery, East Huron 700N: to look at Michelle Kiem's photographs. Hour-long exposures taken at night, the works resonate with light: train lights float above El tracks, a blurring of movement, trace of travel, a residue of presence. Airplane lights decorate the sky, their movements held in place, a latticework of protection. Some people find this work optimistic, for me its beauty seems objective. Within one hour we have reached 37 South Wabash, our destination. The train lines overhead, Karen gives me a gift, a prize for finishing the walk, a small square box, with an inlaid wooden design of the world.

THE FACE OF LOVE

B. C. Brown

The purpose of this memo is to introduce Love ™'s new logo design and provide guidelines for its use.

Reasons for Designing a New Logo
Through research conducted with current, past and potential customers, we learned that our present logo has acquired associations of unreliability due to its design, which is based on the human heart.

As you know, the human heart suffers from poor engineering and is prone to mechanical failure. The coronary arteries, through which its source of blood must flow, are easily blocked have no back-up procedure.

This can result in overloads on the system, often with considerable, if not permanent, downtime. While we've attempted to troubleshoot the situation, we have not been able to find a viable fix.

We have also found that due to these unfortunate circumstances, customers attribute undesirable states of being—such as "heartache" or even a "broken heart"—to our product.

We are therefore abandoning our current logo for a more robust image.

Presenting . . . The "Quad"

Short for quadrangle, "quad" communicates reliability:

- Structured after geometry, not biology.
- Excellent building block for a good relationship.
- With a firm base and fewer stress points, it is less subject to breakage, failure or pain.

Quad stands for:
Quality • Utility • Amor. • Durability

Implementation . . . Where and How Will the New Logo Be Used?

Here are just a few examples of its implementation:

Expression of affection for one's Schnauzer will change only slightly:

I  my 

becomes

I  my 

An expression of love for Mary remains an expression of love for Mary:

becomes

And in cases where more emphasis is desired, previously indicated with an arrow, we suggest the addition of an affirming check mark:

becomes

Please contact your branding co-ordinator if you have any questions.

BLOWJOB

Kevin Sampsell

She said she was going to give me the blowjob from Hell. So we found a place to park on the way home. It was a cemetery. She said her cousin had given her boyfriend the best blowjob. She said they talked about it at work. She said she told her cousin that she was going to give me the blowjob from Hell that night. It was a competition.

But who is to judge which oral sex is better? I thought about asking but decided against it. It would imply that I wanted a blowjob from her cousin. I'm not sure if I would have disputed this, her cousin giving me one. They were different types of women. So different that I wondered if they would even be friends if they weren't related.

It was going good there in the cemetery. It was an act she prided herself in, like how she was proud of her tits. I liked her tits. They were small but good. They had a shape. Friends of mine had seen her tits and said that they were good ones, proud ones.

I didn't last long enough. She seemed disappointed in me. Maybe we both had an idea in our heads what the blowjob from Hell would be like, and how long it would last. It wasn't to be.

When I started the car and pulled back onto the thin winding cemetery road, I ran over a couple of small tombstones. We were stuck for a moment, but then the ground became more solid, and we drove off. We looked at the dark landscape, with all its concrete teeth sticking up and poking out of the ground. The ground so dug-up and reapplied.

Song to the Siren:
Damon & Naomi
on tour with Kurihara

SUB POP RECORDS PRESENTS SONG TO THE SIREN:
DAMON & NAOMI ON TOUR WITH KURIHARA
A TWO-DISC SET: LIVE CD & DVD TOUR DIARY
DOCUMENTING DAMON & NAOMI'S 2001 EUROPEAN TOUR
WITH MICHIO KURIHARA (GHOST, WHITE HEAVEN)

AVAILABLE APRIL 23 SUB POP DVD SPCD 592 www.subpop.com www.DamonandNaomi.com

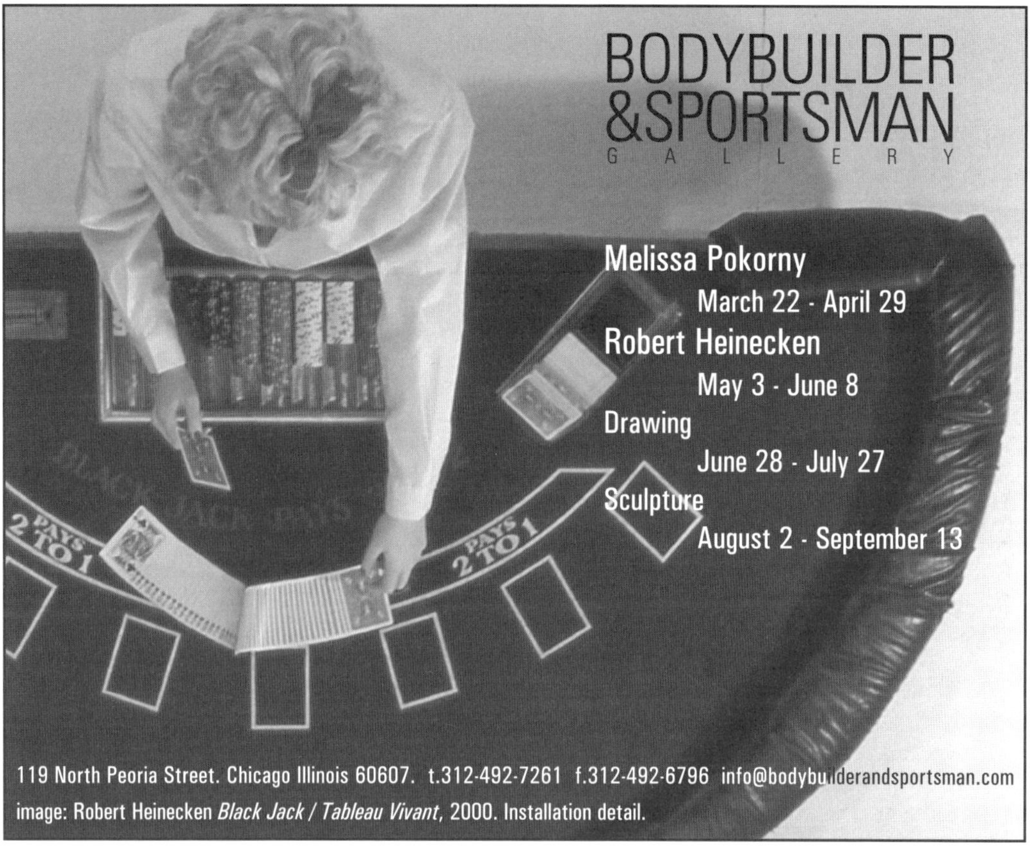

Melissa Oresky
opening march 29, 6-10 pm
march 29 - april 27, 2002

Beth Reitmeyer
opening may 10, 7-11 pm
may 10 - june 8, 2002

STANDARD

1437 n. bosworth ave. chicago, il 60622 773.486.1005 saturdays 12-5 or by appt. www.standardgallery.com

FLOTSAM & JETSAM

by Aidan Higgins

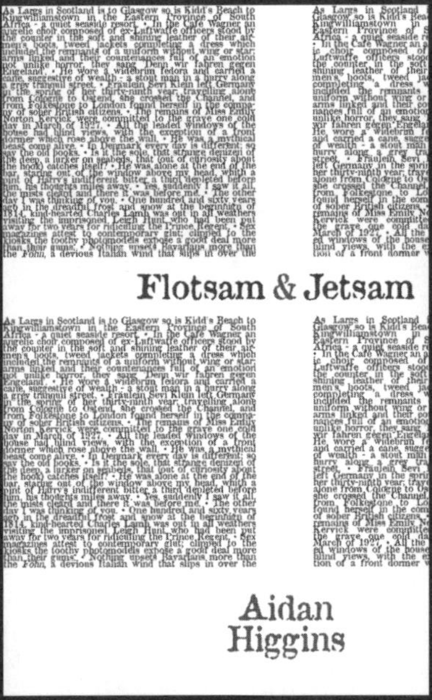

• • • IN STORES NOW • • •

SHORT FICTION | $15.95
1-56478-316-2

"*Flotsam and Jetsam* offers a vivid illustration of Higgins's range and eclecticism, his outstanding control of atmospheres, his literary development and his importance in the history of twentieth-century Irish literature, in which he can be seen as a missing link between the modernist period and contemporary writing."

—*Times Literary Supplement*

Aidan Higgins is one of the most highly respected Irish writers of the past fifty years, heir to such master stylists as James Joyce and Samuel Beckett. The short prose and fiction collected here spans Higgins's entire career, and provides American readers with a compelling introduction to a major international literary figure.

www.dalkeyarchive.com | DALKEY ARCHIVE PRESS

INTERVIEW: ALEX SHAKAR

Michael Workman

Michael Workman: How do you think your experience of Chicago contributed to your writing of the *Savage Girl*? As I read your descriptions of Middle City, I didn't think of *Chicago* so much as I did, say, Iowa City.

Alex Shakar: That's a good question. It's funny how everybody has their own idea of what the city is. I originally started off taking actual streets from different cities around the country and incorporating them into the book and then it gradually stopped being that literal. But I did take a few things from landmarks in Chicago. I lived right on Division Street near Mary of Nazareth Hospital and every night I'd look out my kitchen window and see this icon—it's replaced now with a new one because they sold the hospital to somebody else—but there used to be this icon of Mary of Nazareth standing there with this blank circle for a face and hands at her sides, palms forward, and it was supposed to be a gesture of welcoming you with open arms but it just looked like a shrug. *No insurance, no service*. So that made it into the book—you could also interpret the "middle" in a lot of ways; you could say it's middle America . . . there's something purgatorial about the city.

MW: Or maybe even the average American. Your graduate studies seem to make an appearance in the *Savage Girl* as well, most notably in Chas, the fallen-from-grace Philosophy professor.

AS: My experience with academia gave me the ability to research this stuff in a way that I might not have . . . Chas's lecture on irony, for example. I ended up studying what a lot of people had to say about irony and what these academic types had to say about marketers because they're an interesting breed, these trendspotters. A lot of them are self-taught—they're a lot like writers in that way—some of them come from business backgrounds, others come from academic backgrounds. The way that they're partly cultural anthropologists and partly businessmen, they've got one foot in either world but beneath this there's this urge for a community. I thought they would be a great metaphor for the kind of searching I was doing—for my attempts to find meaning in popular culture, in these throwaway surfaces of trend and fashion that we all take for granted to be meaningless. There is something about these trendspotters that's a lot like what writers do, in that we try and find a meaning in our contemporary moment; you're able to look at life this way and find something. The epigraph by Baudelaire is such a great allegory, the prose poem about the "Bad Glazier," this guy who's living in a ratty hovel, this misanthropic guy. You don't know whether he's an artist, a crazy guy or a bum or something and this windowmaker walks by on the street and says to himself, "Well, let's play a little joke on him," and you don't know whether he's serious or not or joking then he looks through his panes of glass and he says to this guy, "What, you have no colored panes? You have no panes of paradise? No blue, no red, nothing to make life beautiful?" Then he sends him away and shouts down at him, "Make life beautiful!" and drops the flowerpot on his head and shatters the glass. Just that cry, "Make life beautiful!" we rely on. Just the sadness of that image, that we rely on a window to make our lives beautiful—we sort of do and we don't. In a way, we all hope we will, that we'll find some sort of pane of paradise, whether it be a work of art or a product and I think that trends and fashions are the lowest form of art—and by saying "the lowest," I don't mean to make a value judgement. They're the simplest and most popular—the most rudimentary maybe—forms of art that people have access to, such as how they express themselves through their fashions or through their purchases.

MW: A kind of basic utility or instrument of self-expression? As opposed to an attempt to make art, people can wear a company logo to feel connected to something larger than themselves—fashion, consumer culture and the advertising that promotes them serve as reminders in a way, reinforcements of a certain perspective that the companies that these trendspotters are working for are attempting to mold and sell along with the products. I read the idea of "paradessence" as based on desire, on the idea that the paradoxical essence of a product should present a consumer with something they both want and can't have, with the paradox being that no one person can live either option instantaneously.

AS: I guess I was saying that we expect a kind of magical operation that different products perform for us, that we do want them to do mutually exclusive things for us. I myself don't side with Javier or with Chas—for example, Chas, the more cynical one is the guy who says that paradessence is a way of tricking people, where for Javier it really is a way of giving people everything at once, that we buy into these things and it actually does make our lives better in some way. I think that's sort of the meta-paradoxical thing about these products is that it does both dupe us and our lives are made better by them at the same time.

MW: Because we're buying into an illusion?

AS: Because we're buying into a conception of reality that is as real as we want to make it.

MW: A reality that becomes Javier's ultimate product, a selective reality.

AS: That's the basic question at the heart of the novel—how this increasing tendency of our culture to express itself through our purchases—does it either give us power or take our power away? I think the book ends up in the middle, saying that really, it does both of these things. Because I think consumption in a very real way is power, but in another way is powerlessness. Aside from making you feel better, making you feel freer, making you feel like a different person or something like that—aside from that feeling of potentiality it might give you, it also gives you very real things—like social status, that's a very real form of power. But it's also a very delusory power in terms of what you're putting your priorities into and what you're spending your money on and what you're actually getting for your money.

MW: Again, a parallel with the author, in terms of being able to create and sustain an illusion.

AS: Yes, that's true. Good point. Like, for example, right after September 11th when the politicians all came out and started telling us to go out and shop…

MW: And were pushing for Trade Promotion Authority as a means of waging war…

AS: I mean, they're not wrong in that consumption is power, and that we can grow our economy but it's also in a very real way powerlessness for us as a country in that it makes us more dependent on our material desires, makes us more dependent on supporting dictators for the sake of oil and ravaging ecosystems for the sake of food. My book is also about that paradox of consumerism on a more personal level.

MW: Consumption also seems to placate in terms of our interest in civic responsibility—if you have these things, then you're provided for and why then feel that you need to participate instead of simply going along with some immense tutelary force that's providing you your direction?

AS: I very much think that's a crisis people were realizing as our war against terrorism was unfolding, that this conflation of citizenship and consumership—there's this increasing public will to believe they're the same and that's a new thing. I don't think anybody ever thought of them as the same thing. I guess what Ursula discovers in the course of going through the book is that every attempt at being a citizen is shunted into consumerism and that we live in a society where more and more, the only act anybody can commit is an act of consumption and that's the only way we can express ourselves or that's the way we're encouraged to express ourselves politically, spiritually, emotionally or whatever—through consumption. That's what I mean when I say a delusory power, that's where it gets fatuous in our will to believe and gets to an extreme point where—in an earlier draft this was a little bit more explicit—where Chas says that a future American democracy will consist of shareholders rather than voters and power will be apportioned depending on how many shares in the country you have. It sounds like an almost logical proposition when you break it down and think about it.

MW: Our modern electoral process, for example. Let's talk a little about the sources for your ideas about consumerism as an instrument for cultural steering.

AS: When I started thinking that I wanted to write a book on trendspotting, I read everything I could on the subject and I was looking for a philosophy that I could put in and I ended up having to make it up myself, like all that stuff about paradessence, because I couldn't find anything that cool or that insidious out there. But, I did find something that was pretty chilling and that was—the father of consumer motivation research, Ernest Dichter, as I talk about in Chas's lecture—in the introduction to this book he wrote called *The Strategies of Desire*—what a wonderful title—this was when the Cold War was really gaining speed, in his introduction he made this comparison between American marketing and Soviet propaganda, and he said that on the surface, both of these things appear quite similar; if you look at American advertising and a Soviet propaganda poster, you'll say, "What's the difference?" But, in fact, they serve opposite functions. This is his defense of America consumerism: he says that, in the Soviet Union, propaganda exists to create contentment, to make citizens feel like they're part of a Great Society, to make them feel good and make them happy with what they've got, whereas American marketing exists to create perpetual discontent and make people always want newer cars, bigger houses, younger and more beautiful spouses. But, this was his defense of it, he said: this is what's better about us, this is what's always going to ensure that we have the economic advantage, because we're always going to be pushed forward in ever-progressive manner, always discontent and therefore always working harder to get what we want. He said that's what was going to win us the cold war and eerily enough he was borne out—I really think you can say this was true, that's what won us the Cold War. But, thinking about it, if our culture is based on discontent, how does that affect us and what does that mean for us? After I got to that point, I started walking around and just seeing the world in a different way and everything—reading, looking at advertisements or walking to the supermarket—I just started paying attention to what was having an effect on me and why? That's when I came up with the idea of paradessence, that there is some paradox in every product trying to promise you mutually exclusive things. Since then, the marketers who have read this book have said that this is absolutely true and how come nobody's described this and at that point I got scared.

MW: One thing that I kept getting hung up on was how the savage girl is essentially a homeless woman, who seems to have entirely rejected social engagement. In a way she's a caricature of rugged individualism—and then I found myself trying to connect that with what Ivy was trying to do, so that for me the savage girl eventually became two people who exemplify distinct types of lifestyle solutions to the problem of consumption.

AS: That's a good way of looking at it. They are different expressions of the same social problems that I was trying to get at. Ivy's what happens when you clean up the dirt, but both of them are empty in a way. I wanted to be very careful to avoid any romanticization of the "noble savage" as an alternative to materialism and consumerism, to show the lie behind that too.

MW: Right, there's no such thing as a "noble savage," since nobility is a civilized concept.

AS: Another paradox—that's also why we end up where we end up in the book, in the jungle, and we see what happens when you have this romanticization of getting away from consumerism and that's the alternative. I really wanted to show that that wasn't the answer either, that you can't do what the savage girl does, that her rebellion isn't going to be an effective one in our culture.

MW: Your image of the volcano comes to mind here too, which I read as a symbol for Modernism or how our modern ideals necessarily operate with an ignorance of natural forces in action and often in reaction, as with Ivy's schizophrenia.

AS: Sure. I think it serves as an image of all the things that our culture's trying to pave over in a way that the people in the city don't even acknowledge as something that's happening in their lives that's going to blow up. That we live in a world that's very much in danger in a lot of ways. I was thinking a lot about literary modernism when I was writing the book. Pound's statement, "Make it new," is something that artists for the whole 20th century, and still, have taken as a given of what you have to do as an artist, you have to make it new. That slogan could almost be an advertising slogan, so the concept of newness has just become so co-opted by the concept of novelty. In the same way, I was reading Emerson awhile ago and he says something like how every man should make of his mind a temple to change—and it's such a great statement because what he meant was a temple to the great men of history who have done great things. But when you read it now—

MW: You think a temple to celebrity.

AS: Right, which is what we are in a way, so this notion of newness being turned into novelty and celebrity—this a book in a lot of ways about irony and about how irony, which was formerly a tool that artists had recourse to in critiquing society—they could write satires of society and maybe even effect changes with that because it would be disturbing—and when I started out on this project I was very aware of the fact that it would be very difficult and probably foolish to write a straightforward satire of consumerism and a satire of the marketing industry because the marketing industry has to such an extent co-opted irony so that now it's an industry that pretends to make fun of itself all the time. And so, all these tools that we had, these notions of literary greatness, of some kind of probing irony, have been to a large extent co-opted by an all-consuming marketing industry. These little attempts at rebellion are taken and remade so that the meaning is taken out of them. Artistic rebellions are also incorporated so that, for example, if you hear a piece of music or see a painting style in a museum, within a week or two it will be in a commercial and its context will be changed and it will be harnessed to power this industry that you're trying to critique. So, I knew that I was walking a very fine line and that I'd have to make a delicate balance between irony and earnestness—hence "postirony." That's why, when I was at a marketing meeting at Harper Collins, they said "this should be a textbook for a marketing classes! We should market it to marketers!" I just had this vision of my book once again being co-opted into this machine—which is what happens with Ursula's work, which is a marketing campaign itself and hopefully since I've written a work of art and she did a marketing campaign, I will avoid that fate.

Dogmatic: (noun) the first place to look for the last thing you would expect to see. Synonymous with great Art and great ideas since 1997.

Featuring works by Yuki Kokubo James Leonard and Julia Marsh through july

1822 S. Desplaines
312.492.6698

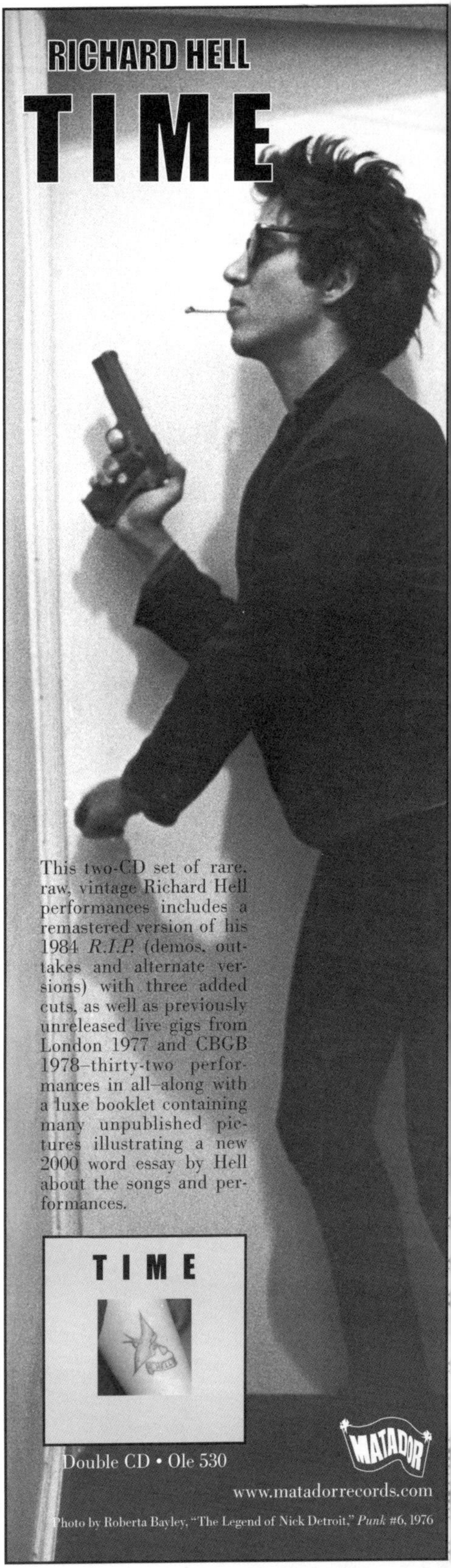

your surroundings illuminated

ideoTech Imaging printing gallery open-end art

2130 w division 1e chicago 60622 773.278.2818 m-f 9-5 weeknights-end by appointment

LOOKING FOR MR. G BAR

D. A. Powell

shapes repeat themselves.   and messages rewind
it's the answering machine you don't want to hear from

"I could never be kept," he says.   the fear of sobriety
wets his tongue: slips it into my ear with his number

sitting in prospect park bar: conveniently contained
by the lack of scenery. his shorts creep up his leg

hand: too casual.   considering his inner thigh
parts of the same body arouse each other: kissing cousins

we all sleep with men who are not our lovers: economically
the barter is proposed: more drinks on the mastercard

the pitch and roll of a bed crosses my mind.   how to end
this groping beneath the formica table: nobody walks away

I used to wake beside the same body for years
its contours familiar: until it no longer suited

who knows where desire goes when it leaves the bed
a stranger comes to sit with me: we both light up

he's had a lover test positive. his lips find my neck
his hand, his ass: I consider the risk of each part I want

there is a covert exit.   a cab waiting.   I sign for us both

"MR. SONG"

Mr. Joe Meno

I lived next-door to Mr. Song. Yes, the one from the radio show. At the time of our acquaintance, we had struck up a kind of arrangement whereby I would leave small paper bags containing decorative bottles of various grain alcohol and fruit liqueur in front of his door early in the evening, say around 8:00, right before a bachelor goes out to, say, pick up his date. Then, after a cheap movie at the Esquire or some dinner downtown maybe, I would come home and knock on my neighbor's door twice, then bring my date into my own crumb-bum living place and allow ourselves to wait. Slowly, I would be engaged in dimming the lights, arranging the pillows on the sofa, drawing the best devilish smile I could without trying to give a hint, and then, surely and soon enough, there would appear . . . just like that . . . enchantment.

Margaret was a girl I hardly knew: one big, beautiful red-head whom I had met at a small cocktail party hosted by some bum at work, work, being the no-account consulting game, whereby ingenious stiffs like myself toil to save plutocratic institutions from shelling out any more cents of their workers' pensions than they have to pay. At my job, I was an absolute no one. A complete zero. I could walk down the maze of rows and rows of tiny white cubicles so much like bordered compartments of some senile, money-hungry heart and no one would recognize me. If I ran into my boss or my department supervisor on my long tours around the office, there would always be a moment of awkward silence where they would try to remember my name and when they never could, they would say, "Good job on that Abramson report," and I would nod, because in that business, the business of nickels and dimes, the business of the future interest of a penny, beauty laid in the soft configuration of numbers and not in the telling features of some stranger's face.

I, on the other hand, have always been more interested in the esthetic of certain, unknown, beautiful faces. Margaret was a looker with red-hair that spilled down her back like the most glorious tropical volcano explosion you could ever hope to discover during a holiday. I was watching her the whole night; the way she was holding her drink, a vodka and cranberry, some cocktail maybe, and spilling it slightly while she was smiling and laughing, which was a good sign, because that meant that she was actually smiling and laughing and not one of those kinds of gals who will talk your head off and smile and laugh when they don't mean it because you certainly haven't said anything funny and there's nothing worse in the world to me than a gal that's a phony. Around mid-night, when the party began to break up, and Margaret the red-head was climbing into her soft, fur-collared jacket, I

pulled an old one, which every lousy Ivy-Leaguer knows but thinks is too shameful to use, but I figure if a trick is old then it has to be good. I approached and crossed behind as she was pulling her arm into her soft white sleeve and zip-zap, she ended up spilling my wine all over me and staining my sweater and, oh, the spoilage, oh, the humanity. Margaret, the dear, was all red-hair and full of the most beautiful silver apologies, and "Will it stain, you think?" her voice like choir bells as she asked, and me, being chivalrous, replying, "It's no matter," and her saying, "Well, it's horrible of me, I'm a horrible person, really," and me saying something swell like, "No, it's horrible of me that I should have upset you like this," and her closing the deal with, "Well, here's my number and address, please promise me you'll send a bill," and me, unable to take my eyes off the freckles of her neck the whole time, simply stopping myself from smiling.

(There is a box of clothes I donate to the Salvation Army on account of this stunt every year. Dry cleaners have wanted posters of me in their back room, I swear.)

Margaret, being a girl I caught on such an old trick, was sure to be charmed without end on the first date. Candlelight dinner, walk in the park, I touched the darling, most innocent path of her white wrist and remarked what a beautiful watch she was wearing and left the petting at that. In her heart, she must have been crying, no, singing, thinking what a gentleman, what a catch I was myself, but really what a bum. What a lousy no-good bum I am. And I mean it, friend.

Margaret was more than happy to see me on a second date. The second date she wore something off the shoulders which was a kind of easily-translated message to me. I was an old tube radio, no, a foreign correspondent, I was sage was saying, "Tonight, more than anything in a thousand years of waiting, I want you to kiss me." So I did. In front of a fountain with a silver statue of Neptune in the center of it. I took out a quarter, said, "Did you know this fountain is magic?" tossed the quarter in, told her to close her eyes and then I kissed her. Before she could argue, I said, "See it works! I got much more than I could have ever wished for," which ended with more kissing and her sighing, then lying her head against my neck in the taxicab on the way back.

At this point, I must argue, on my behalf, that clearly, clearly if a girl was so gullible to fall for both of these ploys, she must have been either a chiseler, a tramp, or a nun. A chiseler, well, whatever they get they deserve, I say. If a girl is simply after your money-clip, then whatever turmoil they create, they've made themselves. I've been with women like that and the horrifying thing is the similarity they share with men who have one thing on their minds, an end, men like the kind I am, I guess. A tramp, well, a tramp is a sad kind of girl on her own and it's usually best to steer as clear as possible, only because, though they may not be lacking in fun, they always end in some kind of car-wreck. A nun, well, a nun. Margaret might have very well have been a nun; the kind of girl who is raised by nannies and spends summers with rich relatives in guarded estates in the country. Necking to her might been the real thing, truly. Going on looks, she was a knock-out but it seemed within her beautiful head there could not have been anything but very lovely green vapors and I guess, I didn't know what else I should have expected.

I made a mistake, is what I am saying at this point, I guess.

On the next date, our third date, I left a pint bottle of scotch in front of Mr. Song's door just before I went out and on the way back in with Margaret, gave the indicative two knocks, took her fur-lined coat, coaxed her to the sofa, whereby the clip of flame-red hair came undone and my heart swaggered like a love-drunk sailor. It's in moments like that where I doubt everything I'm doing, the games, the tricks, etc., etc. A moment like that, with the hair tumbling down the shoulders, will make you forget everything. But then you remember the hair clip being removed and your date slowly removing her shoes is just some other kind of trick of their own, and has very little to do with comfort and a lot more to do with, simply and effectively, enchanting you.

At that moment, more than anything in the world, I began to pray that Mr. Song would begin his singing, because I was swimming. To be honest, with the shoes off and her bare feet inches away and the red hair lighting a fire along the sofa and her asking, "Are you all right, darling? You look flush," well, I was swimming. I asked if she wanted a drink and she nodded and I stalled some more, mixing the highballs. Just when I felt about ready to settle down permanently and kneel at this beauty's feet, silence hung in the spaces behind the thin plaster walls with such heavy weight that I felt matrimony nearly setting in. There was still no singing.

Usually Mr. Song starts out with something tender like, "That Old Feeling," sure, something nostalgic, not too serious, capricious, yes, but full of the definite implications and intentions of love. Wherein, I would, feigning surprise, declare, "There's my rowdy neighbor, Mr. Song, howling at the stars again," and stretch one long arm around the victim's neck, then ask, "Did you know he had his own radio program in the 40's?" Then there might be a nice interlude, a procession into "It's Always You" or some delicate Gershwin, "Long ago and Far Away", where my fingers would begin to toy with the string of pearls around the young lady's neck, Mr. Song's voice rising, growing more powerful and much more brassy like a trumpet shaking loose some of its dust and rust and by the time "Time after Time" was slowly sweeping through the tin vents and cheap plaster from the apartment beside mine, clasps would be unclasped, boundaries would be surpassed, and a soft cooing would be heard as a kind of accompaniment with each of Mr. Song's carefully chosen lines.

And still, it went very wrong the other night.

Margaret, no dumb nun as I had guessed, caught me giving the two knocks on Mr. Song's door. I covered as best as I could, saying, "It's a sign we have. He gets worried about me, he's like a grandfather, I guess. I wouldn't want to keep him up all night waiting for me."

"Could I meet him?" she asked.

"Oh, he's probably indecent at the moment," I said and she just shrugged, and gave the old man's door another few knocks, until the rummy came to the door, shaking his scotchy head, as confused as me in his bath-robe, I guess.

"Hello," my date smiled, "I'm Margaret." Just like that, shaking his hand.

Mr. Song looked at the girl, then at me. His face was white and soft with the lines of a bumpy pillow along his forehead. He had yellow whiskers on one side of his face and a blue vein along his knob-nose, which was purple as a beetle. He cracked open one red eye, which was like parting a mussel from its shell and muttered, "I'm ready," and then, "Is it show time yet?"

Very quickly, without thinking, I said, "Well, I didn't want you to wait up for me. I'm home all right. So you can . . . go to bed, old pal."

"Good," he said and closed the door quick and then that was that.

When we entered my apartment, I began stalling, trying to think of something to say, waiting, waiting, hoping, praying that the old man would start singing anyway. But there was nothing. There wasn't going to be anything tonight anyway.

Margaret began to kiss me, very softly on the mouth. Margaret did not wait, she began to unzip her dress and I worked to unclasp her brassiere, gently running my hands along the top of her freckled chest. I felt like an adventurer embarking on a most beatific snowbound expedition, but without the supplies or resources I needed to pass the test and just then I wondered, *Here, here is a girl who does not need tricks. Here is a girl for me.*

I went along with it all very quickly, beginning to unbutton my pants.

"Would you put a record on?" she asked. "Something soft."

"OK," I said. I got off the sofa and put on a Cole Porter record, letting the music slowly build in its blueness. I dimmed the lights and took a seat back on the sofa, giving her a smile, still hoping the old man would give us one song for experience anyway, but it did not matter. All the quiet things of the world were beginning to blossom with love right before me.

"I am trying to be brave," Margaret said.

"You are doing very well," I said back, kissing her arm all the way up to her neck.

"I am being very brave," she said again and I looked up and saw she was crying. Small soft, tea-cup-shaped tears were gently riding down her cheek and I leaned back, not knowing what to think, because from the way she was going, I was pretty sure of one thing: Margaret was no nun. She was something I had never had in the apartment before, I think.

"The other night. In the fountain," she said.

"Yes?"

"I wished for this."

"So did I," I said and for the first time all night, it was the truth, which was a real moment for me, bum that I am. The record began to skip and I sat up to go fix it. When I came back to the couch, Margaret was trembling. In the soft crook of her elbow, her pulse was beating like a hidden rabbit and I realized very quickly that I did not have the sincerity to handle something like this. We began to kiss again, and she was lying there, nude on my sofa, and I was beginning to undress when I heard her say, "My brother died. In the service last year," and it was a real queer thing to say, especially at a time like that. "It makes me see things. Things that aren't always there."

And so I began to realize this girl was seeing things, things that were the lies of things I had planted and things that were no good and I just sat there and she kept on kissing me, whispering, but I just let the music block out any words she was saying and I was stiff as a corpse and she was asking me what was the matter and I just listened to Cole Porter blaring out of the hi-fi and then Margaret was yelling, and cursing at me, and I just stood there, in the dim lights as she began to dress and within a moment, the soft fur-collared coat was back on and I was watching Margaret climb into a taxi and the red hair was disappearing, behind the glass, down the street, around the corner and out of time and out of reach, for me, at least. I walked back upstairs, knocked on Mr. Song's door, and found him in empty bottles, lying on the floor beneath a flock of white moths. Without a word, I lifted him gently along the neck, dragged him into bed, and shut-off the light. I sat in my apartment and stared at the walls, listening to him breathe, thinking; then finally watching the city awake from the tranquil spell of night, wondering exactly what I was doing and how alone I was feeling. I thought about making a phone call to someone but I could not think whom to call and I sat like that, alone, thinking, until the entire room was filled with light, and there was one thing, one thing I kept saying over and over again, in my mind:

Margaret.

I never meant to make you cry.

Three Poems

by Joyelle McSweeney

The Premier

On a wave of resignations and dismissals without precedent
I rode in. I drove in from Connecticut. I was called in.
I sanded down graffiti from the door
of my concert box. I took the sixth seventh and eighth floors.
I stood out under the red tree and opened the preferable flesh.
I took the eighth ninth and tenth. I was deeply
in love with the building. Stings the cuts on my fingers,
rinds against my toes. A fat brown leaf
into the red minnowy leaflets drops and stops dropping.
They look down at me. A tenterhook adapted
from the linen trade, a cartilaginous collar: I rode in.
If you can't chase down your butcher for a cut of white king,
see me. If you're from hell, you're from hell, see
Fat leaf at rest in the still red tree see me. Who am
I if I mean what I sometimes mean.

INTERVIEW WITH A DOG

After three nights on the mountaintop, the dog began to speak.
The night sky curved around to hear

miel, honey, mille, the thousand flours, mildly

What language is he speaking? He needs dog friends—

My sheep were nervous in the passionless state.
I'd made it halfway to the goldfields
when my vehicle burnt to the ground on its own.

when the SWAT team formed a diamond and sunk into the canyon floor.
Wedged in the dripping crevice, I watched the circles spread

knowing the right one by its soaring expense.

This is a great apparatus for the United States,
here in the Superdome. What created light?
My master's spoken word.

I've been so sick and sad about this dump forever,
making lamps for the Vatican of design firms,
accounting for, abluting,

parading outside the city wall with my crew of wild turkeys,
and my Map of the Waterholes, Lava Flows,
Dune Seas, Cinder Cones,
and Organ Pipe Cactus National Monument

and my folder of languages and temperate zones

The house-dog pleads for his liberties and mercies
Padfisted, reeling in my trunks—
this torso wants out!

Light squares off . . .
I stand at the bell for the winnowing out
The hymn-dog whispering
accounting for, abluting
this mark food left on my body
this mark a dark thought left around my eyes

and the loss of my white sheepbodies
and what was tied so tightly to my wrist

Joy

1. sees everything in its place, including herself.

At the equally secretive
Institute for the Brain: Joy; a bomb-plot
at the Radisson hotel; a file of phone-bills
from the local cell.

The Jordanian plot is the *template*.
The Jordanian account is *accurate*, or so
officials have been persuaded.

Joy the Mortarman. Joy the American.

2. known only by her nom-de-guerre(s).

A fuse; a bulb in the mail. Above the double-hulled
basement shell, Joy buries the bulb in stones.
water blubs down. A leaky cask.
A flammable lake o'er the concrete bed
spreads. We walk above it.
Somehow, it doesn't ignite.

3. Joy; blub; The dreaming arranged
and the forged Gold Dealer's License
to avoid detraction, and the four separate routes to avoid;

and the bellwether perched on the little rise; one
of two hooves; ruminant; a grassy fall

4. *Rehearsal*:
Placards banging our chests.
Mine says *The Precedent*.

There was a house held up by plumbing.

There was a chimney house.
As we threw over it in the heliocopt.
As it happens, there were various skeletons
(of houses) and a dozen ties
and shirts in the back of the Chevrolet.
And there would be a deliverable inaugural
in exactly that many days.

5. the consciousness of a break, actual or impending.

Seated before the cerulean tank.
If there are criminals at all here, they're in the balconies.
And one in the front row waiting for a sign

6. actual and impending

Sleep Passages
In a finished world, sleep could not be waking.
could not be *distinguished from*
waking at noon. *nein*, nine.
Non-consuming.

7. wake up to the auction of a doublebird jar.
sleep through the auction at the armory.
The beautiful antique lances
tilting into new lucky hands.

8. A three-part command to stand.
And if not, a command to stand.
And if not, a lifting.

9. A victrolling of my single, novelty hit . . .

10. And meanwhile, seated before the grid,
at least we gave the country what it wanted.
Lush crepe-covered blackouts
roll down the coast. Still, seated before the dolphin show,

separated from our *conditions of origin*
from a sense of *immediate living*
from the *genius loci*

or whatever

And then the grid explodes

11. And meanwhile, old chrysanthemum-head,
health-happy!
And meanwhile, old cormorant keeper,

Joy

Discover the Writer's Life in New York City

Faculty 2001-2002:
Jeffery Renard Allen, Hilton Als, Donald Antrim, Deborah Brodie, Peter Carey, Jill Ciment, Jonathan Dee, David Gates, Lucy Grealy, David Hajdu, Zia Jaffrey, Jhumpa Lahiri, David Lehman, Pablo Medina, Honor Moore, Geoffrey O'Brien, Dale Peck, Robert Polito, Francine Prose, Sapphire, Dani Shapiro, Laurie Sheck, Jason Shinder, Michelle Spirn, Darcey Steinke, Benjamin Taylor, Abigail Thomas, David Trinidad, Susan Wheeler, Stephen Wright.

Visiting Faculty:
Ai, Martin Asher, Frank Bidart, Margaret Gabel, Glen Hartley, Dave Johnson, Phillip Lopate, Thomas Mallon, Glyn Maxwell, Robert Pinsky, Lloyd Schwartz, Jon Scieszka, Ira Silverberg, Tom Sleigh.

Director: Robert Polito

Master of Fine Arts in Creative Writing

Over more than six decades of steady innovation, The New School has sustained a vital center for creative writing. The tradition continues with our MFA in Creative Writing, offering concentrations in fiction, poetry, nonfiction and writing for children. Study writing and literature with The New School's renowned faculty of writers, critics, editors and publishing professionals.

Fellowships and financial aid available.

For a catalog and application
Call 212-229-5630 ext. 322
Email nsadmissions@newschool.edu
www.nsu.newschool.edu/writing

New School University
The New School
66 West 12th Street New York NY 10011

GOOD FOOD

flo

LOVE

312/243-0477

1434 W. Chicago Ave. • Chicago, IL 60622

Intelligentsia

Carefully selected green coffee beans roasted daily in our vintage German machines.
Proudly poured at Chicago's finest restaurants.

FRESH ROASTED COFFEE
PREMIUM FANCY TEA

mail orders 888.945.9786

3123 N. Broadway tel: 773.348.8058
www.intelligentsiacoffee.com

Girl Games

Caitlin O' Connor Creevy

"This is a bunch of crap," I murmured, unlatching the velcro on his soft bondage cuffs.

Flabby Mr. Hatch, his arm now dangling over the side of the bed, faked as if he wasn't in terror, but he was a human in captivity. Every breath of mine was a new combination to a safe he would never crack.

"Give me money!" I demanded, staring at the ceiling, knowing my tiny boobies were killing him.

"I don't have it," he said.

I stared at the chintzy jewel box on the black lacquer dresser. I knew there was a real brooch inside, a rooster with a missing eye. Mrs. Hatch had worn it to graduation when Isabel and I were at Locke . . . The rooster had had both eyes then, but.

I didn't want his money.

I slid on my crocodile short-shorts and antique Save the Whales halter which I had peeled off with such gusto two hours earlier. But the coke had run out. In the final analysis, S&M made me yawn, especially with a noodle like Hatch.

I took the brooch. He saw me do it. He just turned his back to me, laying naked in a twin bed, fifty, with welts covering his white body. Welts that he was willing to pay for with Mrs. Hatch's mother's sapphires. I threw the brooch at his back, hoping the needle would dig.

"Ahhhhh! Jesus God!"

I walked out the back, the rickety screen door screeching shut, no black rubber air cushions to soften the sound (maintenance being a low priority at the Hatch's). I walked through the suburban alleys surrounded by superstore debris and dusty food bags and boxes, half-chewed by dogs, still barely eaten. Abandoned toasters. Hubcaps from Nissan Sentras. Dumped comfy clothes. I made my way through the trenches of Grove Street and Downey Drive and Camden Court rubbing my eyes, looking for butts, swearing. It was sunny and cold, and it felt good to me once I gobbled the handful of vicodan I had smartly stored in my sneaks. I was full of treasures. In my shorts pocket was a fun-sized box of m+m minis, the contents of which had been reduced to one crackly clump. Better that way.

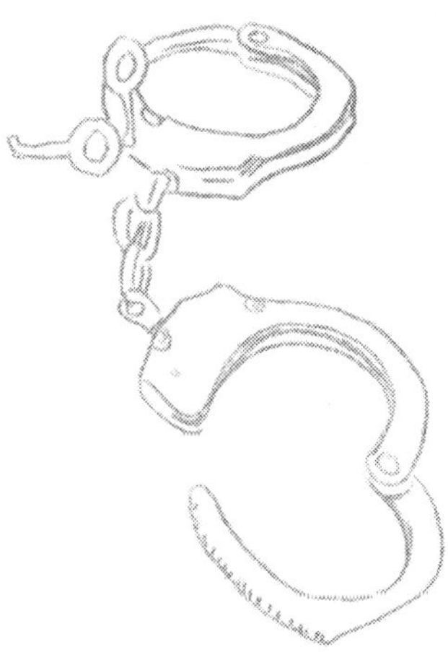

"Take that" I hissed, slapping a big plastic garbage can with my whip before ditching the cheapo dominatrix prop inside. I turned the corner and walked out onto the main drag.

I used to think that these suburbs were real. OK, those feelings were twinged with disgust and condescension, but once upon a time I thought that people who loved their kids lived here. Overweight people who kissed boo-boos. I must have been twelve when I thought that. When my own parents were doing the paperwork. My feelings for Mark Hatch had been intense and real and now they were dead. They were intense. Now - dead.

I pulled out my phone and called cabs: ABC . . . 123 . . . Best . . . Better . . .

"I'm standing in the parking lot of Bank One on Dempster . . . hello? Between Dunkin Donuts and," (I squinted my eyes to read the miserable sign) "Lighting Plus."

"Five minutes" they all said before clicking.

I really just wanted to get stoned. But if mom was awake (unlikely- since she kept the schedule of a koala, aided by a regular overdose of Ativan) I would have to raid her pills.

Better swerved into the lot like a Palestinian gunrunner. Best had gone into D&D for a cruller. "This is Better" I thought, and stepped inside the car. A man named Mamoun, according to the identity card on the dash, was at the rubber-studded wheel, getting a massage from about fifteen different directions, wooden roller balls on his back, faux fur on his bum, a fan on either side of his headrest and God knows what underneath the hot pink silk pajamas he was playing off as outerwear in broad daylight.

"227 Bank Street," I said.

"Chicago." he replied, as a statement, not a question, and I knew that everything was smooth.

I drifted in and out of sleep in Mamoun's two-toned taxi. I was dreaming about a white ghost scrambling eggs when he screeched in front of my house. I handed him some bills and stumbled out of the car, zipping my pants as I walked up the path. I made towards the door with my head jutting forward like an ostrich on the run; I was thinking about the bathroom when I reached the side of the house.

"Mother!" I exclaimed, genuinely surprised to see my middle-aged mom standing at the door wearing an expression which seemed to say "we're all gonna die."

"Your father is here," she informed me in a monotone.

I said nothing. I was equally shocked.

I walked in to the living room and stared at him sitting on the couch admiring our latest issue of *W* magazine.

"Hi!" he said in a loud voice, looking up at me.

He was wearing a baseball cap from Camden, Maine, cocked sideways, with a fat stomach couched in a soft Brooks Brothers shirt—nehru collar, and wearing high-tech flip-flops. "Who is this person?" I thought.

My God, he's a corporate wigger.

I saw him last ten years ago with a tan canvas briefcase slung over his shoulder as he walked out the door. That door. Right there. I looked at the door.

"What is he doing?" I thought, and the realization came to me: "He's taking the money away."

"Ann! Buni and I want to invite you to dinner," he said.

My absentee father and Buni, his sixteen-year-old wife, wanted to invite me to dinner. I turned to my mother.

"I think you should go," a robot said from inside her throat.

"OK . . . " I guessed.

"Well done!" he said, as if I were a disturbed child who just answered the final question on a remedial aptitude test, which itself was being tested for disturbance-sensitivity.

I looked out the window. Bright, but shaky. Clouds passing, trees rustling, honk honk. He looked out too, and hummed.

"They said Californy is the place you ought to be" I made out as his song, and then he quit, and I picked it up in my head.

A gust of wind blew open the window and the iron hinges squealed, a supernatural confirmation that we were, in fact, standing in the middle of a scary movie. He looked around the Great Room.

"Just too chilly here," he said, as if Mother and I weren't there, as if we weren't picking up on what he was saying. That Mom is a bitch. Yeah. So she is. But she's a good bitch loyal to the core, you rat.

My mother looked at the front door. I looked at myself in the mirror. I could see my mom in it too. We were strange. We were weirdos with the same beautiful eyes. Our eyes were so beautiful, we could victimize.

"I understand you've just become a father. Congratulations," my mother said to him. I stood there and observed their dynamic which I hadn't witnessed for so long. She wanted to kill him. That much was clear.

"Thank you, Lila. Buni and I . . . " he made a motion towards his pants like he was going to pull out a picture, or a sonogram maybe. But he changed his mind, and just patted his back pocket, giving his wallet a little pat . . . "are overjoyed."

There would be no more questions from Mom, just the acknowledgement, just the 'fuck you' to my dad. "You've just become a father." He didn't even get it.

The three of us stood there for a moment before we all began shuffling toward the front door.

"What about you, Lila. Any developments? Anything new in your life?" he asked.

"I'm going to quit smoking!" I interjected like a half-wit, trying to deflect the bullets.

My mother's pencilled eyebrows raised. I thought she was going to laugh.

"No, Mills. No developments other than what you see here," she said looking around the room, scanning over the breakfront filled with her great grandmother

Exie (my namesake)'s bone china, over the blood red sofa stuffed with horsehair, over the dogwood carved cane tilted against the wall. Yet somehow she was centering all of us on me. The product. The development.

Our guest could not resist the opportunity to comment on the décor.

"Hmm, well, you haven't done much to it," he said, of the house, "although these curtains—very—orange—you needed to get these imported?" he said in an awful, phlegmy way, tugging at and then releasing one of the six gigantic golden tassels which hung from the valance, enjoying the feeling of the soft French threads falling through his fat fingers.

We three stood there a second thanking God we had lived separately all these years; it was, perhaps, a therapeutic moment.

"We'll buzz you at 8 . . . " "Dad" said to me as he bolted out the front door.

Mom and I stood dumbstruck. I thought this might be our inaugural mother/daughter drug binge, but instead she asked me in her deepest Mississippi whisper, chin slightly lowered, eyebrows slightly raised.

"Coca-cola?"

"Yes" I replied quickly like the modern day Yankee I was, a pretty girl who had never received a letter grade despite $500,000 worth of education.

She came out carrying a tray with two glasses of ice and two pre-opened cans of diet coke, fizzing, as well as a handcrafted chips-and-dip platter containing rotel and low-fat tortillas. I sat down on the long cream-colored sofa and watched as she made her way into her plaid chair, adjusting the cushion, smoothing the back of her hair, the seat of her slacks. She sat.

Mother held the clicker like it was the soft aged hand of a nursing home patient. She turned on the television. We watched a rerun. She turned off the television.

"Do you think you should get ready?"

It was 6:00.

"It's six o'clock," I said, crunching into the last corn chip, licking the salt from my lips. Mother stared at the empty platter. The grandfather clock in the library started to gong, a little reprimand for my tone. I might have told God to go suck an egg, but never once had I talked back to her. I was her life. She had given up her life for my life. I had to pull off this bs tonight with my dad.

I stood up and started the ascent to my room. I twisted up the staircase, grabbing the hard black bars, wanting to pull them off and put them in my body. Make myself into a creature with metal arms and legs.

"Get ready." I thought to myself out loud.

I could not face my California Closet. I didn't even have the energy to steal my mom's drugs.

I went to my large stash, unzipped the one-zip and breathed in. Buxom red buds, my buds. There was a lot of pot in that bag, but what was I going to do when it dwindled? My "father" appears out of nowhere, stinking up my house like smoke from an electric chair. Did he think it was time to teach us another one of his lessons? Lesson number one: Marry for money. Lesson number two: Dump your wife. Lesson number three: Take the money and run.

I opened up a bottle of nail polish and placed it by the bottom of the door, then set about preparing my bong, a porcelain Chinese man's head with hair on fire that a fun fairy from the Ivory Coast had given to me at cooking camp. I packed the bowl. I needed to beef up my bravado with a billowing high that could carry me through this important night.

I laughed as the word "daddy" crossed my mind. For kicks, I pulled out my old portable record player and listened to my childhood soundtracks. I tried to spin and scratch—I wanted it to go "your bot bot bot bot-tom dollar" but I couldn't get it to work so I pulled the piece of plastic off the record player and smashed it. The whole show made me feel creepy and good, such a common emotional collusion in my life nowadays. I smoked to enhance the natural combination of icky and poz, harmonize my twisted head.

I looked at myself in the mirror.

"I. Love me."

Bong hit.

Bong hit.

I doused myself with a scent my grandmother bought for me at a perfumerie in New Orleans, a little boutique, not of this time, that from the moment you opened the door, made you feel as if you were toying around inside a pink pair of French bloomers.

Inspired, I laced myself in a corset I ordered over the phone.

"He's come at last," I sighed.

I dressed in a purple tube dress, put an armful of gold bangles on and felt with-it and heavily perfumed.

I had watched him age on the flaps of the ridiculous books he published, *The Power of You*; *Become a Realizer*; *Lasso the Moon* . . . the best-selling trail he blazed while wheeling and dealing behind the scenes of Self -Help setting up a post-men's movement men's movement which revolved around specially formulated vitamin packs. He encouraged men to bust out. Escape the tedium of taking out the garbage. In essence, he gave them a psychological green light to abandon their families. He used television. Very popular, became an empire.

"How do *I* become a realizer?" I wondered as I took one last bong hit before I tottered downstairs, hesitating on the last step.

Mother was in the kitchen sipping Fresca from a straw. She looked at me from head to toe. She set down her cool drink, not allowing a single ice cube to jostle. It was as if nothing mattered. We were having a moment of surreal honesty, she knowing I was a fried egg, me knowing she was knowing, us both at his mercy. It was as if we were already in our new life. Our new life where his money was gone from us and we could just fall into lunacy head-first, possibly relish it.

No, we couldn't do without.

My bracelets jangled as I ran my fingers through my silky hair. I sturdied them by pushing them firm at mid-forearm. It was a power move. I felt in control. So what if I was wearing ten thousand dollars worth of hooker's threads. What was ten grand—a used car? What if I were naked in a custom gold jacked-up Chevette, with illegally tinted windows, revving like a hyperactive beetle in the middle of the kitchen, terracotta tiles crackling underneath my booming system. It was 7:50. I considered going back upstairs and changing into a black skirt. Did I smell? I sniffed myself. Mother pretended not to look. Good Lord, I was stoned. I smelled like a flower, though—the nectar of great fields of verbena and honeysuckle pressed onto my pulse.

There was a loud rap at the door.

Mother answered it and he entered. Our house. His house.

"Mills."

"Lila."

He looked at me from head to toe.

He wasted no time. (He was a realizer.) "Andiamo," he said in an American accent and charged out the door.

I followed.

We walked out into the 50 degree summer night, the click of our shoes echoing on the stone path to the car. We were alone for the first time in a decade; we looked straight ahead, at the car. A big black driver held open the third door of a stretch Landcruiser.

"My God," I thought.

I sat alone in the row behind Buni and "Dad," black man in command at the helm.

In the rear view mirror I could see the driver's wraparound shades, which he wore with a puffy gold-flecked safety strap.

"This is a fun car." I said.

No reply.

My father finally nodded to acknowledge my comment; he turned to me.

"Why don't you have a car, Exie?"

"I don't drive."

Buni perked up, "You don't know how to drive? How weird! I mean, that's just, like, so . . . " she trailed off.

"Buni, that's Exie's prerogative."

"Why do you choose that?" he asked me. "You could need those skills in a life-threatening situation."

For a second I got a little worried. I might be in the Sahara, travel mate fainting from exhaustion, leopards approaching, Gila monsters on the windshield. I grabbed a cigarette from my purse and *zehhhhhhhhh* opened the window of the fully-loaded vehicle.

"Excuse me—" my dad said to the driver.

The driver pulled his shades down the bridge of his nose; his eyes turned towards us, and his head followed slowly, obediently, like a snailshell being dragged. He was driving full speed ahead with his entire face to us.

"You are a professional driver. My daughter needs to learn how to drive. I'd like to arrange that."

"Oh my God," I thought, smiling, horrified. To be embarrassed by your dad. This is what Isabel must feel all the time.

The driver looked at my Dad as if to say, "What you talking bout?" His shades skied down his nose and dropped to his big tummy, suspended by the safety strap.

Dad nodded.

Buni stared at my face.

I dug through my bag for a light.

We arrived at Sach's which was literally three blocks away; it was absurd to have driven, and Dad impatiently waited for the door to be opened. He flicked out his presidential-looking watch and glanced at it twice before first Buni, then I, got out of the car. The watch game was his coping mechanism, curbing his urge to knock us out of the way and bound out of the vehicle. I remember the gold monster Rolex he had when I was little, how he would pluck it, and breathe heavily out of his hairy nose. I would watch the little rectangles expand and contract on the elastic tightropes around his wrists.

When I was six, Mother went down to Mississippi when my grandfather was dying, and Dad and I were alone (except for Durla, my voodoo nanny); and he had to pick me up from ballet. I was trying to change on my own in the girls' dressing room after class. From my low vantagepoint in the dressing room filled with tutus and mommies, I saw my father's gold-wrapped wrist wrap around the door. I couldn't get my arm out of the top of my leotard. He tapped hard and loud on the door. "Time to go," he said from the waiting room. "Time to go." I really couldn't get my arm out and my shoulder was turning red where the neck part was pulled so tight. I tried with all my might and I was so frustrated; it was so hard not to fall apart.

"Goddamnit," I heard him say under his breath outside the door, and he walked in. A woman came over and looked me in the eye. She popped my arm back into my leotard and she said, "Just go without your clothes, sweetheart." And my dad grabbed me by the hand and we left. "There, that wasn't so hard, right?" he said. "Let's go." It was freezing, but he wrapped me in his big trench with fur inside and we got into the car running out in front.

Sach's was half-empty. The hostess was sneaking bread in the coatroom. White and kelly green linen topped the tables, brown men hustled under control with silver crumbscrapers; sweet-trolleys rolled around on wheels with just a hint of a squeak. Sach's wasn't born yesterday. On the east wall, the mural of Chicago was chipping with decorum. I was scandalously stoned. It was time for a grown-up drink. Maybe a Campari. Yes. A Campari.

The carvings of trees on Sach's old brown walls could register as scary when the candlelight flickered.

Buni looked like a claymation sorceress. She had clearly been under the tutelage of a pagan midwife.

"Buni, that's a fascinating brooch you're wearing."

"Um."

"Your brooch—your pin there on your blouse. It's funny. I always think of old women when I think of brooches—but you're not old at all, are you?"

We were escorted to our table immediately.

My fleshy father got up to wash his hands. He returned toting our drinks from the bar.

"Excellent!" I thought, "we're all alcoholics!"

Buni took a self-conscious swig, dribbling onto herself. "Oops," she blubbed.

"So, Exie!" "Dad" shouted, "we would like to talk to you about the future."

Better yet, why don't you just explode right now, and take your drunk little gryphon with you. I downed my cocktail with profound efficiency.

"We have a child now," he shouted.

What had connected my mother and father in the first place?, I wondered.

"We have been thinking," he continued.

Buni slurped around her glass. She truly was not paying attention.

"But let's order another drink," he thought out loud.

No sooner did he say it than an erect-standing man was at our service. All three of us looked at "Paul," the clean, yet residually oily waiter, an eerie fifty-something lifer in the restaurant business, undoubtedly the renter of a small, still apartment far away from here, in which limp pasta was regular fare.

Dad drew a lasso in the air with his finger; Paul tacitly expressed understanding, and round two was underway.

"I take care of my children," Dad announced.

"Mmm hmm," Buni added warily, rocking back and forth a bit, like a restrained worshipper. I felt warm, and looked around, hallucinating for a moment that we were in one of the wooden churches of Natchez, Mother's hometown.

"I like to take care of my children," Dad continued.

I stared at the pattern on my saucer. Egg. Dart. Egg. Dart.

"Let me ask you something, Exie. Are you taken care of?"

"Taken care of?" I repeated, looking up from the eggs and darts of my china.

"Daddy," I sighed, "you take such good care of me."

Dad commenced a coughing fit. Buni handed him a glass of water.

"Mills?" she prodded him, breathless.

"You take care of me, it's true. I am eternally grateful for my education, and that Mother and I can eat so beautifully," I said, buttering a sesame thin, looking around again for the waiter.

Buni got things going, "Mills says your mother's people were slaveowners; is that right? I mean, that's not bad, well, it is, but it's not your fault."

"Excuse me," my father uttered, through a forced reprise of his hack, and got up to go to the men's room.

"I'm sorry. That's so long ago," Buni blundered. "That's like, a hundred and fifty years ago. We were studying about the civil war at school when I got pregnant. My history class was going to go on a field trip to a civil war reenactment, but you know . . . I'm sort of into the muskets, though, and the cannonballs. I wanted to see those bags of gunpowder. Those leather bags?"

I packed my American Spirits.

My father returned and sat down, which signaled me to talk about my mother.

"In 'The War of Northern Aggression,'" I began, "My great great great grandmother's family owned a plantation. They had a hundred slaves, twenty in the house, eighty in the field. They thought that black people were not as high up on the evolutionary chain, if you know what I mean, but they still loved them. Actually, I'm an octoroon - didn't you know? And what about your forebears, they were...missionaries?

Sarcasm did not ruffle Buni's feathers. "Yes, they were missionaries . . . in Maryland! How did you know? My mother's family, that is. I don't know as much about my dad's family. I'm really into genealogy."

"Genealogy," I repeated.

A waiter appeared and we had another round, as well as a smattering of smoked fish—salmon, tuna, and sword with little wigs of parsley.

Buni suddenly came to life after the brain food. She went on quite a bit about siphoning, the latest tubal health procedure. I wondered if she had frozen her placenta. Maybe they would will that to me. That would be my take. "And Buni's placenta will go to Ex, in hopes that menopause will be a joyful reminder of Buni."

"So what did you do with your placenta? " I asked her.

The room was suddenly quiet, with only the low-decibel clinking and clanking of the restaurant around us.

Clearly this was an uncomfortable subject between Buni and my biological dad. Buni looked down, sad. Dad interjected.

"That is a private matter."

"Oh," I said, waiting it out.

"I wanted to make a soup," Buni mumbled.

"Don't get started," my Dad rumbled.

"The soup has many powers I've heard," I added, encouragingly.

"Silence! I am not going to indulge this table!" my father said.

I was now almost drunker than I was stoned, and I was pretty fucking stoned.

A moment passed where we all sat in an unnatural state of fear-shame, myself at least, on the brink of a giggle.

Breathe, breathe, I thought. But I started to worry about my cilia, which I thought I might be burning with French exhalations. Neither of them was smoking. Were we in the non-smoking section?

"What do you plan to do with your life?" he questioned me.

"I'm thinking about law school," I bullshat.

He had to let that one sink in. "Hmph" he said, tilting his head to one side and spearing a fish bit which he then expertly crammed into his face.

"Is that . . . . " he continued after an extraordinary pause. " . . . true?"

I put out my cig on my bread plate. It made a chilling, soft whine as it rubbed the china.

I speared a bit of fish myself. "Mmm-hmmm," I resounded. I was having difficulty swallowing, overcome with nausea, as a sliver of tuna woggled out of the corner of my dad's mouth.

Buni was overwhelmed by the menu. Dad's was already face down. My nose in my own, I mumbled through my elimination process. "Soufflé - no, nothing eggy. I do not want a steak. Freak it, I'll have the rabbit." Buni looked at me with doe eyes. I stiffened my resolve and placed my order with Paul.

"I'll have the Beef Wellington," my father announced, and it was here that I saw my father's cowardice in full flower. A little piece of meat, however good, hidden behind layer of layers of dough, bread, filling, nothingness. Is that being a realizer?

Buni asked what the vegetarian entrees were and ended up settling for some makeshift Mediterranean bowl of babyfood. We returned as quickly as possible to the inquisition. It was a whorl of punitive questions mixed together with helpful hints in a blind stab at being parental. How were my grades? Had I taken the LSAT? Did I need him to talk to somebody at U of C law school, he was sure he knew *someone* on the board. The main course arrived. I noticed that Buni was getting softer and softer as my dad's entire being grew. She was actually blurring out as he was getting sharper.

Then we got through the layers of flaky pastry and hit the meat. The blood was filling up his face and his cheeks and jowls were inflating, creating an overgrown red blowfish effect. He was sawing at his delicate food and pushing back his black hair, which looked crazy.

"Exie, I just can't rectify in my mind what you're doing with my money. It's reckless. I get these bills. I mean, this just has to stop. You'll exhaust the fund in two years. I just don't know if..."

In that moment, we crossed the bridge over lost paternal love into the end of duty, and I knocked my own glass (let's call it half-empty) onto Buni's lap, which was itself in a soft state of post-natal decrescendo.

"Oh God!" I uttered, wiping the Compari off of Buni's white, raw-silk drawstring pants. Buni, ignored, just patted her pants and looked around desperately for Paul.

"You've really depleted your personal resources," my father said to me, spitting violently. "You seem totally discordant, dyspeptic, polarized. To put it frankly, you've got your head up your ass."

"Hogwash!" I shouted, echoing Meredith Baxter-Birney's poorly delivered line in a Lifetime adaptation of the true story of a poor woman from Arkansas who beat her husband. "Hogwash" I said again quietly, hearing myself echo.

We were rolling now, and I was blotto. My dad, having given Buni his napkin—maybe to wipe the pathetic look off her face, started to scan for Paul, too. The lull signaled me to plunge.

"So Buni, did you, like, just start your period and then, whoops!" I asked. Buni looked at me like I was speaking in tongues. I continued, "Does my Dad buy your tampons at the store? Or 'did', I guess. Dad, are you like King Charles, like, 'I want to be your tampon?'"

Then I pinched Buni's cheeks, pretty hard, I guess, because my dad had to slap my hands off her.

"*What?*" I said like a teenager. These were my teenage years with my father, encapsulated in the third course at Sach's.

"What in the hell did you just say?" he asked.

"We talked about that," I continued. " My therapist. My period. My blood. Menstrual envy. That was a theory at the time. My dad left us because he was jealous of my tampax." I laughed hard and started digging around in my bag for cocaine. "Dad, you're a fucking asshole, did you get that bill?"

"I can't believe what I'm hearing. You are out of your mind. You are absolutely . . . This is . . . "

"You should get a refund then, that was like, a lot."

Dad, volcanic at this point, flagged down Paul and got the check.

"Buni, I love you." I said to her face. "It's like, I want to kill you, squeeze you like a water weenie and just squirt you."

My dad picked me up by the arm and started dragging me out, Buni's pitter patter behind us.

"Is that how you feel? . . . Sort of like you want to just squeeeeezzze her?" I asked my dad, blowing a cloud of smoke in his face, obscuring the maze of blood vessels.

"Put that out," he said. "Put the cigarette out. Put the cigarette out!" he said, shaking. "Buni is allergic," he quaked, "to cigarette smoke!"

Buni was crying.

"Buni, don't be a puss," I sloshed.

I limply watched as he paid the check, collected our jackets and threw them over his arm. He shepherded us out and stuffed us into the big gold car.

"Give me that purse!" he howled at me once we were in the car, and grabbed my handbag. He dumped it out: cigarettes, ClearEyes, a little bottle of herbal mini-thins, which I picked up,

"I was looking for these." I said.

. . . a bag of jellybeans,

"Hey!" I yelled when I saw the jellybeans and snatched them.

"What is that ice pick of a mother doing to you?"

"I'll kill you if you say another word about her, you fucking deadbeat dad," I said, eating the beans.

"Driver, she won't be needing any lessons."

"Ha ha ha ha!" he laughed in deep Jamaican and his shoulders went up and down like the people in cartoons when they solve the mystery.

I picked out the green ones and let them roll on the seat.

Buni was in a state of shock and her Paxil kicked in beautifully. "Why don't you eat the greens?" she asked, like we were having a conversation.

"Because they taste like Aim."

"Do you think this is funny?" my Dad asked, and I burst out laughing.

"You think this is funny. OK. See how funny you think it is when you and your fucking money-grubbing mother are out on the street."

"You mean my mother who gave you everything. Who made you? Is that a threat?" I said, cutting my eyes, pretending to be on a daytime drama.

We were at Bank Street.

"That's a goddamn guarantee," he said. "Get out of this car."

I got out. Buni and Dad sped off. I watched them go out of sight and turn into a blur. I hid in the bushes and called Isabel.

I ate half the bottle of "Ginseng Up!" while I waited - with nothing to chase it! Ugh—God. My mouth tasted like chalk and dooky. There was one green jelly bean at the bottom of my bag and I chewed it up. I needed a little toothpaste.

I had to smoke five cigarettes before she showed up. I watched the people. They looked at the house and they looked at me. They could see my Blahniks sticking out of the bush and they were alarmed. So glad they couldn't see my face and stare stare stare.

"Take a picture, it lasts longer," I snarled. I lit the bush on fire. Oh, damnit. It was only smoking though. I climbed out from behind the bush and flapped out the fire. A German art student with a camera got it on film. *She must be a war correspondent*, I thought.

Isabel pulled up to the bumper of the kiwi VW parked in front of my house.

I watched her lean over the seat and roll down the passenger side window.

"Hey, bebe, wanna party?" she said, smiling.

We drove drunk for a few hours, considering briefly an excursion to Gary, Indiana as I mixed gin and tonics on the highway, then abandoned the plan when we realized we were out of tonic. We turned around just as the radio started to perk up. The classic rock station played Europe *Europe* as we headed back to the suburbs.

Tell me the story, tell me the legend
Tell me the tales of war
Tell me just one time,
What it was like before
Bring me the feeling, right in that moment

"Could you turn it up?" I asked her nicely, and she turned it up very high. I think I loved her really, she was really my best friend. But I had made a monkey of her pa. I beat him senseless. I made him pay to smell my million dollar underpants.

Ninja survive, in dreams I walk by your side
Ninja survive, with you there's no need to hide.

So tell me the legend, tell me the story
Tell me the tales of war
Tell me just one time
What it was like before.

"Everything I hear I think about and wonder why I can't stop fucking guys." Isabel told me. "You need to stick with your virgin deal. I mean, you have got to chill, you know, in some areas that we know and have talked about, but..."

"Pull over, OK?" I said.

"Can you hold on, there's no shoulder. Oh, God, Exie."

I had puked on myself and peed in my underpants. At least I knew I would sleep soundly. *Where were those green jelly beans?* We drove for a while then Isabel carried me in to her house and brushed my teeth. I took off my undies and flushed them in the toilet. I think the toilet started to overflow. Isabel put me on the couch and wrapped me up.

What was he doing fucking me? Huh? What a sicko. Here was his daughter taking care of everyone in the house. And he was diseasing up the house with me. Good I was so out of my mind fucked up. It was the only way I could have slept at all.

I awoke to Isabel and her mother getting ready for the day, and for a moment I forgot where I was. No, I knew where I was. I forgot that I was there with Isabel. I had a flash of total panic that I had been caught red-handed with Marc. Marc. What a disaster. What a fucking disaster. I was black for it. I was sooty. I knew that fact, but I couldn't feel that fact. It's like I felt it so much I couldn't feel it. I lay there on the couch feeling like a sick stone.

"Isabel, where is my hairbrush?" Mrs. Hatch asked her daughter.

Isabel had gotten dressed and while brushing her hair, had fallen asleep on the couch across from me.

"Isabel." God, Mrs. Hatch had a way of making you feel like you were at the state mental ward. She was like a depressed Mexican jumping bean wrapped in a hundred thousand layers of tin. My mom hit the escape button, but Mrs. Hatch seemed to get pleasure out of bottling her misery. She wanted everyone around her to feel how fucked over she has been. Very inconveniently for me at that moment. I put my aching head under the baby blue acrylic blankie I had been rationed and curled myself up to fit the couch.

"Isabel" she repeated. She could plainly see the brush still stuck in Isabel's matted red curls.

"Huh? Oh, sorry." Isabel said, bolting upright. She yanked the brush out of her hair and gave it to her mom.

"It's 8:20. We need to leave in ten minutes." Mrs. Hatch stated.

"OK." Isabel said and lay down on the couch again.

It seemed like morning still. Bright light filtered through the blinds. I could see dust particles in the rays.

Marc was fifty feet away from all of us. We could all feel him. Or, I could feel him. I could feel him breathing down my neck. What a nuisance really, that I had gotten inside this family.

Isabel and her mom walked out the door.

I was trying to find the right position to relieve my breaking back when Mr. Hatch descended upon me.

He kissed my neck and I swatted him like a flea, but indeed a flea - small enough to make it through the mesh of my imaginary swatter.

"We're going to turn this game around," he said.

I could tell he'd been watching pornos.

"Come here," he said, and he lifted my body from the couch, faltering, but lifting me.

"Put me down," I blabbed, virtually catatonic. But something in me thrilled again, and that was a signal. I wriggled out of his arms and dropped to the floor. "I said put me down."

"No, no, the rules have changed," he persisted, driven by preconceived lurid fantasy. And he pushed me onto the bed. Another vomit session seemed inevitable. He must not have minded the remains of the last one still stuck in my hair.

He clumsily undressed me, having difficulty unlatching my new corset. He grabbed my thighs and held them apart, staring. His arms began to tremble as he stared, and he quickly unbuckled his belt.

I was so close to the border of mind and body collapse, sex was actually pleasurable for me. I didn't even mind the abrasion of the 50/50 sheets; and the monstrous mustard color scheme of the bedroom swirled before me in a psychedelic haze that soothed, for once.

Something made me shudder, made my whole body shudder—was this... an orgasm?

"I'm coming, Daddy . . . I'm coming," I slurred and shouted and whispered with feeling - or without, I wasn't sure, as Mark Hatch went in and out of my body.

Five or ten or twenty minutes passed. The bed creaked.

I closed my eyes and saw a new picture of my father in my mind and I didn't know what I had done. He was alive and he was old and I was old now and I was in a black hole.

All the sudden I felt like I was going to die.

I put my soft feet on Mr. Hatch's gray chest and pushed him out of me. I got up from the bed and dressed.

"What are you doing?" he said faintly, talking when he should be silent.

I walked out of the house in a daze.

"Sue him. Sue him. Sue him for every rancid chicken soup for the soul cent. Sue him for neglect. Sue him for the reason I'm being molested by a disgusting thin-skinned old man . . . Sue him for forcing me to be congenial to the child he made a baby with, trying to steal youth anywhere he can find it, trying to sham fatherhood to girls so lost . . . Sue him into the ground."

Quimby's Bookstore
1854 W North Ave
ChicagoIL60622
773/342-0910
www.quimbys.com
QUIMBY'S QUIMBY'S
zines
comix
curios
small press

1468 North Milwaukee Ave Chicago, IL 60622 773.862.4882
MYOPIC BOOKS
One of Chicago's
Largest Used Bookstores
Open Daily
Monday thru Friday
11am to 1am
Saturday
9am to 1am
Sunday
9am to 10pm
We buy books on
Fridays from
6pm to 10pm
and
Saturdays from
11am to 6pm
Discuss Books online or request a Book Search at www.myopicbookstore.com

fig. I

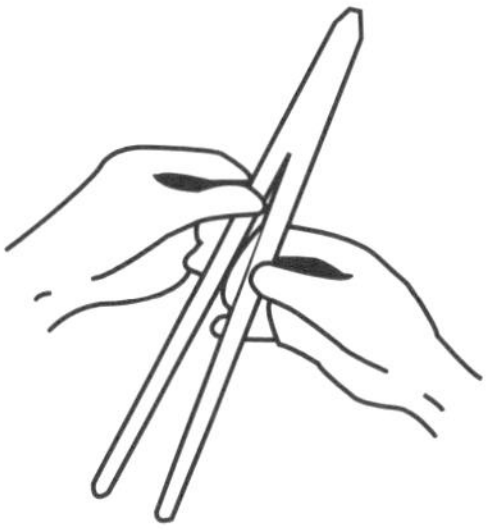

fig. II

fig. III

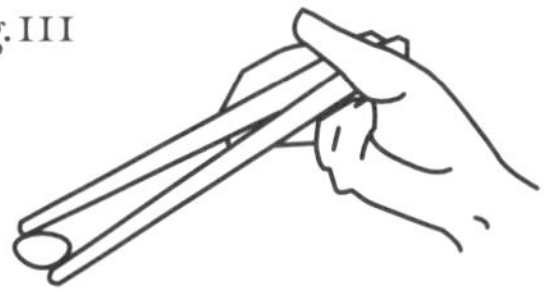

THE HOW-TO ISSUE

VOLUME 2 ISSUE 1 // AVAILABLE IN SPRING

ART + DESIGN + VISUAL CULTURE

TENbyTEN
MAGAZINE

http://www.tenbyten.net

Three Poems

by Peter Richards

Pastoral

To carry on first depilate my body
from either a frictionless or solid position.
From a body renowned with bad overlapping
eggs, a little 14th-century anterior naturally
ejects. Disregard as you would the clear
plasma on a motherboard pawned hastily
by a nurse conditioned to field sorrow
from a predatory and no less fed upon state.
Her name is not Grenadine and though she was
bred to carry the words human-hat power
to the increased and lindrical edge, my own
face resembles that powdery elbow where time
conditions a face to atone once and for Grenadine
the undone circuits of my possible face.
I have noticed living away from each other
tends to encourage dreams of human-hat power.
Plums, bilges, wreaths, intrigues, and the whole
host of spiritual foam left me feeling badly
exposed in the damp glens of helmet ennui.
I know that my deeds (whether good or decided)
can never be enshrined by a new hat's greater hold.
I also know it was not until the human-hat reformers
began the practice of publicly undressing Grenadine
that my own arm was called upon to punish my face.
What my elbow had done for Germany and France,
the human-hat reformers did to my crown.
From hereon hat wearing is enrolled in this book
and I call upon all good subjects to war against it.

WAITING FOR YOU

Endlessness has begun to bore
and makes partial claims at any rate.
Magnification suffers more
than if all the animals were tested.
Each segment an attempt to leave
the vigorous look of machinery
presupposing inert "whereabouts"
where a bradypod secretly mates.
Modular feed announces a buried lens
of murderous singing where blood-mites
prefer paddy lumps to ministered hair.
Primary cones preside in the wetlands
causing a very thin sundress of trouble.
Rakes from the nudity conversion table
dispute Easter altogether. As a rule
Easter is a geometric organ where I awaken
to bailiffs crouching in the center. I want
to emphasize here that one man's wife
is another man's gull, that contours
have a way of saying *I'm not really me,*
I'm not really me, and this booth is enough
for an Anubis statue ingesting himself.

THURSDAY WITH GELATINOUS SHAWL

This new glove trying her honest best.
And this glove stuck to the tongs
held for dipping frightened hair.
Rinsing at home, I did not seek
permission, nor did I serve sincerely
those recruits they asked me to serve.
Hairs skid on the water.
At the very top of the water hairs skid,
and not just because *since* was the word
disguising a bet. Walking home
I can hear home wanting the back room
papered in gloves. I can hear home
washing my body— translucent,
but not really, like a fountain sharing
the milk, or a white dune enjoying my pupil.
My problem is a clear glove
once fixed to the wall turns opaque.
I can't decide if the wall is surfacing
or if the words once used for *home*
frighten each other, holding hands?

NEW ART EXAMINER
ART & VISUAL CULTURE FROM THE GREATER MIDWEST
WWW.NEWARTEXAMINER.ORG
subscribe: 1-800-607-4410
email: examiner@newartexaminer.org
tel.: 312/649-9900
NEW ART EXAMINER
Since 1973.

CHRISTINA

Elizabeth Crane

My apartment is haunted by the ghost of a baby named Christina. I had been living here for a couple of years already when I first saw her, right around the time Joe and I decided to take a break. I think after a year of hearing him plead, *Christina, Christina,* she couldn't take it anymore and finally said, *What?* as he was on his way out the door. Christina is my name, too.

So there's this ghost baby standing there looking up at me and the first thing she said was, *I'm sorry you're having a bad day, man.* Naturally I was a little non-plussed, to say the least, and thought I was surely hallucinating until she showed me some of her special powers, which include scaring the squirrels out of my flowers and giving me blond highlights that don't dry out my hair.[1] Also I'd like to clarify, in my limited experience with ghosts, that she isn't transparent at all, she's completely opaque, although she does have the ability to make herself invisible on an as-needed basis, which you may have already guessed tends to coincide with my attempts to introduce her to people. *I'm not really a people person,* she said.

I hear that, I said.

The last time I went out some lady tried to drag me to her church with some loony idea that she was going to stick me in a manger for the benefit of worshippers wanting to get my blessing, like they do every time statues of Mary start crying or when the face of Jesus appears on a potato. I'm not Jesus, I told her.

I can see that, I said.

Christina told me the story of how she died, (and in spite of what she said, I think she was glad for the conversation) from a fall off the porch about a week after she'd learned to walk. Her mother hadn't gotten into the habit of latching the screen door and out Christina went, exploring, onto the porch and tumbling down the stairs, landing in one of the neighbor's potted plants. *You know that*

[1] I would later hear, at length, about exactly what ghosts could and couldn't do; it was Christina's idea to someday write a treatise on this topic demystifying the stereotypical ghost images in popular culture, which really bugged her. Among things ghosts don't do, I would discover, are walking through walls, carrying chains and moaning all the time (*what's the point of that nonsense?* she said, *there's no* pain *here*); she swore to me that no one she knows would ever have cause to say "Boo." Christina's biggest gripe, though, was the whole thing about "seeing the light" when you die, the idea that there was some big moment of spiritual enlightenment *with angels or some shit,* she said. *That's all crap.*

lady, she said, *the one who takes the pictures of the babies in clay pots, with flowers on their heads and stuff?*

Sure, I said.

Well it was like that, only bad. My mom moved out right away, she said. *She didn't know I was still here.*

Let me make one thing really clear right now. Admittedly, I spend a good deal of time examining the ways in which my emotional and intellectual disposition is unique. But I'm not crazy. This isn't something that's going on in my imagination because I want to have a baby or whatever,[2] she doesn't tell me to spread the word of the Lord, or that there are governmental conspiracies against me (ok, but well, although . . . nevermind); Christina is a real, whole separate person who happens to be dead. The thing about her is that she has this extremely serious look on her face 90% of the time. She laughs and smiles like any baby, *but not unless she has a good reason*. You can easily see her looking around and observing the weirdnesses of the world that a lot of people don't seem to notice. She doesn't look miserable. She just doesn't smile all the time. People have been saying to me, *Smile, Chrissie, smile*, since forever, and it's a huge pet peeve of mine, and I say, *Just because I'm not smiling doesn't mean I'm not happy*. It means I'm not smiling. God. But you know, no one ever believes me. Anyway, so what I'm saying is she has this really serious look on her face, the

[2] I don't know whether or not I want to have a baby *or* get married, as I am certain that I have been culturally brainwashed into thinking that I want to get married and have a baby, and that any free thought I might have about it is colored by all that other stuff, and plus, not having gotten married at this point, when it's getting closer to the time when I will have to rely on technology (and how I feel about all that is another complication entirely) or some other means of producing a baby (theft?) and you know, sometimes these days I'm exhausted just watering the plants.

same way I do in countless childhood photographs,[3] and I could easily see by looking at her that she knows like I do that some things are really wrong. (I know that she can see that some things are perfectly right as well, but I really was having a bad day.) Plus she wears this peach-colored knit dress with a matching cardigan that's cute enough but for some reason it makes her look like an old lady. (Why it is her superpowers don't include a wardrobe change, I can't say.) As it is, she doesn't have that baby waddle. She walks like an old lady, kind of pitched forward, and when she falls down, usually on her face, she doesn't cry, and if you try to help her up, she says, *I'm fine, don't worry about it,* and gets up by herself.

Do you want to tell me what's going on with you? she asked. I told her I was having problems with my boyfriend. She nodded, the weighty nod of a blues singer. I told her that Joe and I had been having some problems for a little while. *He's a decent guy,* I told her, but you know, *he just stays up so late.* Christina nodded again. *And all we ever do is rent movies. And then he says how bad they are, and in what way, and then how bad all the art is, on and on until we've covered the mediocrity of the entire universe, and I'm completely exhausted. We could go to bed so much earlier if he'd just say, "yes, that was a bad movie, all the people are bad, everywhere, good night," but it's never like that.* To be fair, for the most part Joe doesn't take his dismay with the universe out on me, still, it just wears me down. Plus he says "I says" all the time. At first I thought it was kind of working-class sexy. Then no. So we'd kind of decided to take a break. It's possible that he may not have been clear on why. It's possible that *I* may not have been clear on why. It may just have been something to do. I'd been at somewhat of a general loss as to what to do about anything at that point. It may or may not be coincidental that our breakup took place on the first anniversary of my mom having died, and even though I had sort of anticipated that that might be a sadder day than every other day I was also at the same time thinking that because of my unique emotional and intellectual disposition, I would be thus exempt from having these disproportionately large death-anniversary feelings, which it turns out I wasn't.

I bet you miss your mom too, she said.

You knew about that? I asked.

I am *a ghost,* Christina reminded me.

So, what, you're omniscient?

No, she said, *but you know, word gets around.*

Word? What are you saying?

We have some mutual acquaintances.

Well Christ, can you take me to wherever she is?

---

[3]and in home movies, in which any number of great things happen, like riding a tricycle for the first time, which I am clearly enjoying (as indicated by furious pedaling and clapping) in spite of the absence of a traditional facial expression of happiness.

Mmm, no. You can't go that way. Anyway, apparently she moved on a while ago.

Moved on to where? I pulled the curtains closed when it occurred to me the neighbors might see me talking to what appeared to them to be no one.

That part I'm a little sketchy on. There's talk, but no one really tells you until you get there. Word has it it isn't bad. Anyway, give yourself a break. It was only a year ago, she said. My mind wrapped around the word "only" for a little while and I couldn't think of what else to say. *Let's go dance*, Christina said. I thought it seemed kind of inappropriate at that moment, but she stood firm. I want to dance.

Even with the old lady walk, Christina moves pretty fast, so I put on some James Brown. Her dancing is similar to her smiling. She wiggles her butt a little, and then every fourth or fifth wiggle she throws up her hands and waves them around for a second, but there isn't very much more smiling involved in the dance than there is at any other time. I followed her lead, which got a little laugh. I may not have been as good at it as she was.

She hung around for a while. I continued to go about my business but found myself making a lot of excuses[4] to people in favor of staying home with Christina. I liked her. We rented videos and went to bed early.

Christina, I said one night, *do you ever just feel totally different?* For a second I thought she wasn't going to say anything, because the look on her face was enough to remind me who I was talking to.

Then she said, *Are you joking?*

Fair enough, I said.

The thing is, Chris, everyone feels like that.

Everyone might feel like that, I said, *but I really am.*

You're not, she said. *But your feelings are understandable.*

Is that so.

Yes. For starters, you're an only child.

Christina, I said, *I've been through therapy already.*

I'm just saying you have no verification. Siblings, within the family structure, provide a sort of reference. A kind of proof.

You're scaring me a little bit.

I may go into the psychology field, later.

A fine choice, I said.

Further, having lost a parent contributes to the feelings of isolation already in place.

I don't want to talk about that, I said.

---

[4] more than usual, even

You're not a pioneer in this area.

What?

People die. People get sad. You're not the inventor of that.

I'm the only daughter of a somewhat strange and unusual person who died, and no one could possibly know what that's like.

Um. Your dad? Anyone else who knew her?

Not the same. I'm not saying it's better, I said.

You think no one else feels that way and it isn't true.

Shut up.

At that point in the increasingly Pinteresque conversation, Christina burst into tears. I kept forgetting she was a baby, and I said shut up to her and she burst into tears, wailing actually, as babies do. I didn't know what to do really, because it seemed so uncharacteristic in spite of her being a baby, but she eventually climbed up onto my lap and got her arms around me as best she could, sobbing into my sleeve. I rubbed her head and rocked her for a while, and said I was sorry about a hundred times. She finally accepted my apology but again she said,

You're not different. You're the same.

I don't want to be the same.

Ah.

~

At Christmas I got us a tree and dug out my collection of ornaments. Mom and Grandma had made most of them over the years, giving me a new bunch every year in my stocking. The last few years when Mom was sick she didn't have so much energy anymore and started ordering them from mail-order catalogs. I hadn't put up a tree last year because it was so soon after she died and the Christmas spirit eluded me. Naturally, with Christina here this year, I couldn't not put up a tree. Anyway, though, I found this batch of ornaments she'd ordered, little Christmas cookies; snowmen, candy canes and such, that were coated with polyurethane so they could be kept and reused. Except when I took them out of the box, (suspiciously light) they were all crumbly and full of tiny holes, eaten right through the polyurethane by some kind of mealy bugs, those bugs you never actually see but that leave these extensive little empty trails. Christina could see I was upset, and so she made up a rhyme to cheer me up. (*Mealy bugs mealy bugs, you're just a bunch of thugs, you can take away my stuff, but you're just dumb and pasty, because there are plenty of ornaments that aren't so tasty.*) She was a smart baby and her rhymes were good, but she was still working on her meter, obviously, and felt better when I told her not all poems rhyme anyway.

We had lengthy discussions about the meaning of life. I had a notion to write some of her thoughts down, because they were very bestsellery,[5] and it seemed to me like no more suspension of disbelief would be required to receive the wisdom of a dead talking baby than some guy who expects you to believe he sat down and chatted with God. But her ideas were sort of general—she didn't have any better of an idea about what love was than I did. The only point of reference she had was her father (who lasted for a week or two after Christina's conception) and a couple she met after she became a ghost who were killed (in a rollerblading mishap) who seemed truly in love, although she questioned their habit of dressing identically. A lot of the other dead people, she said, were all too happy to be rid of some of their former partners. I asked her if there was any dating in the afterlife, and she said there was, but it didn't seem to be a noticeable improvement.

Joe left a bunch of messages, even though we were on this break. He seemed like he genuinely missed me and wanted to try to work things out. Christina had never met him, but she tried a bunch of times to get me to invite him over; I just couldn't. I hadn't told him about her, and I know he loves kids (although I'm not sure how he feels about ghosts), that wasn't it so much as I just wanted her to myself, even the idea of her. I'm sure the thought briefly crossed my mind that he wouldn't see her at all and wouldn't believe that I did, but honestly I was more afraid that he *would*, and that if he got to know her he might have something I wasn't sure I wanted him to have, and I couldn't explain that to either of them. *Well, at least call him back,* Christina finally said.

I left him a message when I knew he wouldn't be home; it was kind of awkward and dopey. I couldn't think of anything to say. *I'm just calling you back,* I think I said. Naturally he called right back and left another bunch of messages I didn't return, and then he stopped calling altogether for a couple of weeks, which was more of a bummer than I expected, still, I wasn't especially motivated to call him again. Christina and I were having a really good time. Finally he showed up at my door one day with some flowers, not his general thing (he was more of a meaningful book kind of guy), and it was really sweet and I was tempted to talk, but I just couldn't let him in, not having told him about Christina. I said, *I think I need a little more time for me right now,* which sounded horribly hollow and t.v. movie-ish as soon as I said it, and between that and Christina, I felt like he'd think I'd been lying to him. Okay, which I was, but that wasn't our orig-

---

[5] she had a knack for making up slogans – the one she said to me most often was "let go or fall down," which at first I didn't get, especially coming from a baby who often fell down when she wasn't holding on to something, a baby who, you know, died from falling down. I kept trying to convince her to change it to "let go *and* fall down," and she kept telling me I was missing the point, which kind of did take a long time to register. Other slogans included "if you don't like what you see you're probably looking in a mirror." When I pointed out that her favorite, "life isn't so long, you know," sort of contradicted my favorite, "what's the rush?," she said, *Think so?* I guessed she didn't, really.

inal problem, which was him getting upset with me all the time. Okay, which wasn't exactly how he saw it. I might not have mentioned that he wasn't abusive or he didn't call me names or anything, it wasn't like that at all, more like he'd get extremely frustrated because, he said, I kept things to myself. I've always fancied myself a big talker, and I could never figure out what he could have wanted that I wasn't giving him. I told him everything. *It's not about what you say*, he'd say.

When I mentioned this to Christina, she said, *He wants to know how you feel*, and I was like, *But I tell him that all the time*, and she just shook her head. Like she was my mother, but not the mother I had when I had a mother, who would never have butted into my love life. Even if I had mentioned it to her. (Particularly impossible though, when said mother isn't informed that there even is a boyfriend.) *He doesn't know*, she said.

Okay, now, I understood that, but when a baby is essentially siding with your boyfriend, the *ghost* of a baby, I have to say, it's a little upsetting. But I hadn't lost anyone close to me before my mom died and quite frankly, I couldn't possibly have imagined how much it would suck and also, not having lost anyone close to me before my mom died, I would have had no way of knowing that I would instantaneously realize that anyone I knew could die anytime, I would not ever have guessed that I would become obsessed with combing obituaries of any people under retirement age for the word "cancer" (about nine out of every ten), I would not have thought that I would write letters to a dozen astrologists at publications around the country asking them to remove the cancer sign from their forecasts or at least change the name (citing bad karma as my primary argument, which I figured might be a reasonable way to appeal to the astrologists), I might not have noticed that there seemed to be one continuous broadcast about that Tour de France guy who triumphed over his cancer of everything (continuously implying it was some sort of matter of will or something, which I continuously kept thinking, *oh really because I'm sure if they'd informed us about that cure at Sloan Kettering that we would have checked it out*), but a suspicious lack of information about whether or not my bitterness over the entire month dedicated to breast-cancer awareness (the pink princess phone of cancers) was in any way normal at all,[6] I would not have guessed that after someone dies I wouldn't just cry for a month or two and then say well there's nothing I can do, but instead

---

[6] I wasn't so much interested in remodeling our entire calendar to include a cancer-of-the-month so much as I just got into a kind of shouting thing during the interminable month of October, when I began screaming at the t.v. to just fucking cure cancer of everything. I enjoy having breasts, but I'm just going to go ahead and say that my mother, like many people, enjoyed having *lungs*.*

* And it was not possible to convince me, through any kind of rational thought process, that because of the association with smoking that the cancer-curing/awareness/fundraising people thought the lung-cancer afflicted people (the rotary phone of cancers?) got what they deserved when in fact, vast numbers of people like my mother held such an enjoyment of breathing that they never took up smoking and came down with lung cancer anyway.

cry for a month or twelve or more and then also talk to her photos (who unlike Christina, do not talk back), and repeatedly ask her to just come back, making all kinds of deals with the photos, completely believing that somehow via my negotiating with the photos she would actually come back (having no problem at all, at this point, obviously, in believing that it was entirely possible for the dead to come back), I say to the photos, *I know we gave away most of your clothes but I have a lot of your nice sweaters and scarves and I think some of your coats might still even be in the coat closet at Dad's and I will of course give you all the jewelry back and I will give you your car back and all the money so that you can go buy whatever else you need and if you would just come back even for five minutes so I could ask you a bunch of stuff I forgot, I would pretty much do anything* and so with regard to my showing some kind of feelings non-verbally to Joe, I was pretty much thinking well what's the point really? So I can have a long-term commitment with another photo?

I didn't hear from Joe for a while, and I was pretty sure he'd given up until one day when the doorbell rang while I was taking a bath; Christina was listening to Lenny Kravitz and dancing a little. I hadn't been counting on anyone coming to the door, much less that Christina would answer it, and I don't know how she did it, but she got herself up on a chair and finagled that doorknob and there was Joe, no doubt more than a little surprised to see a ghost baby standing there and no one else. I got out of the tub and was reaching for my robe, and when I heard the door open and I heard Christina saying, *Come on in,* and since he didn't run screaming into the street, I guess he wasn't as freaked out as I imagined he would be, and the next thing I knew, there they were in my living room, dancing to "Fly Away." I burst into tears immediately, and Joe took me by the hand and spun me around and we all wiggled our hips and waved our hands in the air, solemnly.

Two Poems
by Joel Craig

The Tree of Life (after Chagall)

Its leaves amplify not one note
but illuminate as autumn converts
a blue suited man.

His blue bride ascends to place him
astride the tree saying "I will part your lips
and your nostrils will be incensed by carnation."

The buzzard accompanist on peanut violin
logs diameter in the moonlight.

With her nymph beak, painter's
palette off-kilter,
Amelia reduces sauce in a pan.

With red cheeks I take her fingerprints.
She has found no solace

from the dawn. It was assembled by ones and zeros
out of darkness and presented as a reckoning
to blue. I wring the dew
from my shirt.

Dim Star is no longer startling,
my jacket always open,
feet bare, I am pushing her with strength
I didn't know I had,
dreaming I've painted
the origin of the galaxy, all the while
ruining stars in tonight's sky.

On The Orphan's Tongue

Unlike a topographical map of the moon, I imagine a blue kiss.

I believe the parrot holds a string in his beak for a reason.

There are too many windows in that bar.

The hole in its window is the crumb of a cloud.

It's an empty effect the dancers have on weeknights.

I would enter this picture of Eden at any time.

With each morning grey Charles disappears.

With imagined blue Amelia rolls back into her blanket.

The flower in my mouth.

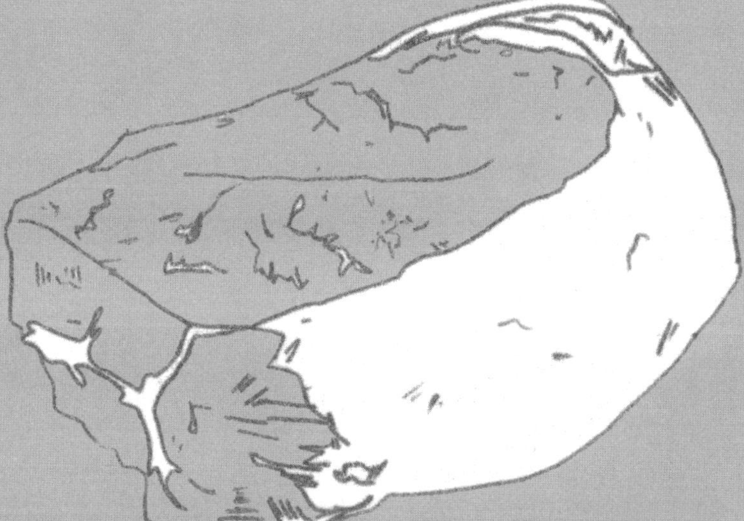

The Pot Roast Consultant

Ryan Kenealy

Thin bloodless strips of beef sizzled in the middle of the table over a small grated gas fire that Keiko tended with chopsticks. She turned the stiffening patches of meat then plucked them from the fire to the plates of Andrew and her husband Yuichi, who let the meat stack as he chain-smoked Hope cigarettes over a mirrored ashtray and conversed clumsily with Andrew about German automobiles and cormorant fishing—things Andrew knew very little about. But Andrew played along trying not to stare at Keiko and the yellows and oranges the fire painted across her clear face as she guided the lever in front that summoned the automated fire to rise then sink between Andrew and her husband.

The waitress returned with a plate of raw caribou and octopus meat centered perfectly between a tight smile and nude pantyhose. Keiko accepted the plate then smiled in Andrew's direction as Yuichi lit another Hope. Andrew could have watched Keiko burn things all night, but he had a conversation to seem excited about and that conversation had taken an unwanted turn to his job.

Bo-eki—Andrew quickly told Yuichi, which meant international trade and sounded better than pot roast consultant. Andrew is a pot roast consultant employed by Rolling Pasture Ranch, Chicago, Illinois. His duties most directly involve the proliferation and facilitation of down home Midwest-style two-kilogram slabs of unadulterated slightly sub-prime Iowa beef. His company's dream for him can be summed up best with a picture: Imagine a quaint old-fashioned advertisement from the fifties, one with an aproned wife bending into a hot oven, behind her stands her suit-clad husband. Imagine he has just set down his heavy briefcase and now smiles behind his freshly return-home kissed wife, his nose bent in the air where wafts the smell of all day slow cooked brisket or rump that's now beaming an angelic glow through the Pyrex. Now go back to the wife who's wearing oven mitts and long red house-dress. She is sliding out the Pyrex basting pan filled with smoking pot roast, colored with carrots and potatoes, and she's smiling the smile of labor appreciated. Did I leave out the kids? The charming rugrats who've put down their toys and stand alongside the dog whose more acute beef-lust is understood, yet the dog is polite because he, like the rest of the family, is well trained. Now take this picture and insert Japanese faces, then you can understand Andrew's mission: the insertion.

Instead of explaining his mission to Yuichi he changed the subject to the weather where he could be more comfortable with his poor, bordering on piss-poor, Japanese. The rainy season ended two nights ago, and everyone seemed happy to see the sun, which now beamed a very wet heat over the stacked concrete of Nagoya. Andrew talked generically about this with Yuichi who looked maybe 40 years old, but had surpassed 60; his wife Keiko was 38. They live next door to him on the sixth floor of a pink concrete high-rise 25 miles from downtown Nagoya. The building stands buttressed by big pink concrete legs over a parking garage that has a spot for every tenant who knows the social importance of driving an extravagant car while living in a pieceofshit apartment. Every unit comes with a balcony caged in chicken wire to deter the large crows that have been feasting on the exposed, powdery necks of little old ladies all over Tokyo—this made the news almost every night: large crows swooping over defenseless old ladies almost picking them off the ground as if they were reverse storks. Andrew, who: owned no car, was too large and too young to be plucked away by the nagoyan crows of death, had enough cryovaced bags of Iowa rump to fill a waterbed; stood at night on the balcony of his apartment to watch the red lights from television towers and dark alleys blink some strange language across Nagoya.

Yuichi had a Toyota Crown Deluxe—brand new, he mentioned, while Andrew poured showa over the twitching strips Keiko set before him. "30,000 American dollars," he said unflinchingly then dropped his cigarette into the thin layer of water at the bottom of the ashtray. The last cry of Yuichi's cigarette and Andrew's reaction of "hmmph" seemed cosmically timed. Andrew offered to pay for the meal but was denied the right three times, which was proper etiquette according to Andrew's guidebook. Keiko took care of the bill with the yen-stuffed envelope Yuichi handed her. Yuichi was old Japanese; therefore he played no part in any monetary transaction—this was etiquette passed down from the Samurai—according to the aforementioned guidebook. Keiko excused herself to the toilet as Yuichi and Andrew walked out the door through the staff's chorus of appreciation for digesting their postcard-perfect raw meat. They walked to the back of the parking lot and sat in front of a small bamboo forest to breath in the dense smoke of burning flesh blowing out the back of the restaurant. Andrew knew they chose this restaurant for him, they knew that he was from Chicago, and therefore he only enjoyed eating the flesh of large land animals. Andrew was not craving the flesh of any large animals, but politely pretended to be when asked. This sort of process happened often.

Yuichi's cell phone rang. "Mooshimoosh," He answered, then soon giggled over sparse conversation. Without warning he handed Andrew the phone. Andrew's Japanese was not great; his Japanese over a cell phone was horrible, being able to see the person's gestures was so important. Andrew said hello and heard a young girl's high pitched voice on the other end. The phone crackled in swirls like they were talking in the eye of a telecommunications hurricane. Yuichi laughed at his new American friend's befuddlement, then took his phone back and said a quick giggling "bye-bye" when he saw Keiko walk out the door.

She smiled when she saw them in front of the dense forest of green bamboo tubes. She smiled this wonderful smile—most of her teeth pointing everywhere but up and down; her eyes pierced. It was an amazing smile that Andrew lost himself in.

The pink high rise was just down the street. During the walk home Yuichi explained to Keiko that he was going to bring Andrew somewhere else as Andrew stared into the window of the veterinary hospital next door. He had to walk by the animal hospital every day, and it always teemed with shaved and mangled dogs and cats wrapped in casts or collared with those white cones. It was horrible to see every day, but completely unavoidable. Andrew watched a young couple in front of the vet; their heads low, they looked tired, emotionally spent. They slowly bowed their heads in unison to some morbid instructions or explanations the vet administered. Yuichi looked back at Andrew then slapped his shoulder. "*Whiskey, ii desu ka?*"

"*Hai*" he said snapping out of the trance the pet-loving couple placed him under. "Ii desu," (yes whiskey sounds good) he responded then bowed to Keiko and wished her a good night.

They got into Yuichi's 30,000 dollar Crown Deluxe and drove through the pink legs of the parking lot. Andrew caught himself doing this a lot in Nagoya, he would just stand around hoping something would swirl around him, he had no pat goodbye, so he was always strung along because people could see something either pathetic or yearning in his eye. A large TV screen in the middle of the dash displayed a map of their neighborhood, a white caret symbolized the Crown Deluxe as it turned through the streets and alleys dotted with red lights sewn into the pavement, and blinking in the darkness. Yuichi drove quickly happy to display the agility of his Crown D. Andrew asked him who the girl on the phone was.

"*Ahh Maki-tyan,*" Yuichi said smiling.

"Your daughter?" Andrew asked which made Yuichi laugh and say nothing further.

They stopped in front of a small dark place that had no sign beside the red paper lantern lit in front. Andrew couldn't read the kanji on the lantern in front of the plexiglass door that Yuichi pushed to the side and quickly walked into the barrage of "*irrasyaimases*" (welcomes), from the staff. Yuichi led Andrew to a table in back of the bar, past a plump Japanese girl singing "Like a Rolling Stone" karaoke. Her eyes were fixed on the prompter screen displaying a video of a waterfall montage around Bob Dylan's katakana'd lyrics scrolling down. Everyone else around the bar drank their beers and ate small fish pizzas without mind to the chubby girl who looked up from the screen to shout the refrain that must have meant something to her *How daws id feeru.*

Yuichi had a waitress in kimono bring a bottle of Jack Daniels. "*Tennessee de kara ne?*"—it's from Tennessee he said, to which Andrew smiled and said *soo desu ne*—that's right. Yuichi flipped through his wallet as the waitress carefully poured the two whiskeys then placed the bottle on the table. Yuichi pulled out a small picture of a young Japanese girl sitting rigidly on a striped couch. The girl was smiling perfectly, her teeth all straight and white. Yuichi, smiling also, asked what he thought of her, and Andrew told him she was pretty. Unsatisfied with the answer, he asked if she was his type. To which Andrew shrugged and said sure.

"You probably don't like Japanese women, huh?" he said.

"No. No. I do."

"You have a girlfriend in Chicago, right?"

"Yes," Andrew said smiling.

"But she is in Chicago," he said again smiling a more mischievous smile, which quieted Andrew.

"You probably think Japanese girls are just cute, right?"

"No, that's really not it," Andrew said then carefully sipped his whiskey.

The whiskey tasted too sweet for Andrew, and Yuichi spent more time praising the quality of the American whiskey than drinking it. Yuichi explained he had to drink slowly or he'd get the red face then dropped another Hope into the ashtray. His cellphone rang again, and he answered then laughed and looked towards a lady walking in. She was the same lady as in the picture. "*Ahh Maki-tyan.*" Yuichi said in a sultry voice into the phone at Maki who sauntered in smiling with her pink cell phone elegantly placed to the side of her face, the antenna blinking a pink light.

She looked more perfect in person. She was thin and angled dramatically; her hair hung low in black waves, so black you could almost see purple strewn in it. They bowed to one another and she put out her hand for him to shake then displayed that perfect smile as she sat down gingerly with her back straight as if she were about to play the piano. She looked comfortable in this posture. She didn't move much as she spoke, she used her round brown eyes the way Yukiko had used the fire—they'd rise then sink to form expression. Yuichi took pride in Maki's presence with more smiles, more laughs. He massaged her shoulder as she made small talk with Andrew. The waitress brought her a pink martini and Yuichi some green tea. Maki took small sips with two hands—one below the base and one along the curved cup. After each sip she'd wipe her red lipstick off the brim of the glass with a linen napkin then turn the glass slightly to the right before returning it to the table.

After the first drink all superficial conversation seemed spent and there they were, three completely different people with completely different lives and completely different expectations of one another. Yuichi would soon run out of toys to display and up until then Andrew brought nothing to the table beside his milky cheeks and hairy American arms. Andrew had no idea what Yuichi wanted from him, but it started to seem like there was something; maybe he was there to impress Maki, maybe he too was a toy for show and tell, maybe it was something else or maybe it was nothing at all. And while it was obvious what Maki gave to Yuichi, the converse was not apparent. Was Maki paid by Yuichi? Andrew was getting tired so he stopped drinking the whiskey, if he'd drank a drop more Maki would refill his glass quickly without asking.

Andrew mentioned that it was getting late and that he had to work in the morning. The thought of work made Andrew cringe. His boss had been berating him through fax transmissions all week. He didn't want to think of his job at the moment. He had failed miserably on his last mission. He drove through the Aichi prefecture to meet with a group of housewives who were interested in receiving pot roast consultation from a young white boy. They seemed pleased to see him and his tall thick body constructed from years of pot roast consumption. Andrew came armed with cooking instructions written in Japanese, cartoon pictures of cows with big dopey smiles, pictures of what part of the cow the roast came from, slanted nutritional information. He even had little diplomas with black heifer silhouette designs on them for those women who could successfully cook the roast. The diplomas sat next to the cooler that held 15 cryovac sealed bags of the finest rump roasts you could find. Andrew stood holding a microphone in front of the ladies, proud as hell with bags of meat in hand. Any of these women could have been model for his dream picture, his corporate goal picture. He held up one of the bagged roasts. It looked and felt gorgeous to him. He bent down and showed it to the crowd for their approval, and they were all interested, they crowded around the meat. One lady had her hand up, and Andrew was praying he would understand her question. "*What is the purple liquid in the bag?*" It took him a little while, but with the help of one of the ladies up front pointing directly at the blood he understood.

"That's blood from the cow."

"Purple?" she asked

"It's purple because there is no oxygen in the bag. If you look at the blood in your veins it too looks purple because there is no oxygen around it, see," he said holding up his arm. But as he looked out over the sea of housewives he could sense the confusion on their collective face. He got out one of his steakknives and cut into the bag, and let the red blood run over his hand, then held it up for everyone to see. "*Aka desu ne.*" He yelled triumphantly with one hand covered in cow blood, the other holding a steakknife before the mob of curious housewives. The scene switched from burgeoning curiosity, which the cowboy music he had playing helped evoke, to utter horror. In unison all the housewives put their hands over their mouths. Some of them shrieked and there Andrew stood, his hand now dripping blood over the cow-silhouetted diplomas.

Maki opened the door of the Crown for Andrew, and they headed home. The car ride was quiet until Yuichi reached into the middle counsel of the

Crown for a blue toothbrush that had only one row of bristles, then ran the brush loudly over his teeth.

Andrew daydreamed over the swoosh of the toothbrush, and somehow unwillingly his head rolled back to Chicago, back to the parking lot of Rolling Pasture Ranch. He remembered talking with Al who worked midnights watching over the dry aging bovine carcasses that would be sent to Japan, where they could demand top dollar. When Al heard the company was sending Andrew to Japan, he explained to Andrew that he needed to show him something. Al showed up every night one half-hour early for his shift. He hadn't called in sick in over three years. He wobbled in, tidily dressed in his polyester Rolling Pasture night-watch uniform that couldn't contain the dank armpit stench that collided with the smell of a bologna and cheese sandwich his wife prepared for him every night and the thermos of discount scotch he prepared for himself every night. Al was a dependable employee who got drunk every night watching black and white security camera footage of dangling cold beef carcasses. "I got something to show you," he told Andrew. "I'll bring it in tomorrow," he said. The next night after Al set his bologna sandwich and thermos on the control panel he walked Andrew outside with an excitement that showed he'd probably waited all day and night for this moment. They walked to his old tan Impala that encapsulated in more dense form the smell of cheap scotch, bologna, and rotting flesh. Al popped the trunk and above the spare, lit by a dimming trunk light, lay what looked like a samurai sword.

"Wow," Andrew said then reached for the sword. Al moved closer to Andrew, looked up and smiled into him with his small yellow teeth. "Go on, touch it," Al said, in an unwanted almost sexual tone.

"Where'd you get this Al?" Andrew asked grabbing the handle, wanting to end this soon.

"WWII," he said slowly then coughed for five seconds: "Pull it out," he said, and Andrew did as was told. The blade was old and dull, but still reflected the light from the parking lot lamps and Impala.

"Wow," Andrew said again, ready to put it away and go home.

"Do you see it?" Al asked—their conversation now almost echoing in the metal trunk of the Impala.

"Yeah, of course I see it," Andrew replied as Al crouched closer and ran his finger, which now held a Lucky Strike, over the edge of the exposed blade to the top where he stopped at a brown blemish.

"You know what that is?" and he continued even though Andrew made no reply. "That's Jap blood," he said bending in the trunk too close to Andrew, bathing him in discount scotch vapor. "I got 'em with his own sword," he said and smiled wider. Al's smile was pulled out of the frame in Andrew's conscious by the sound of moaning within the ergonomically designed cabin of the Crown Deluxe.

He looked at Maki in the backseat—her arms folded neatly over her legs. Smiling her smile. He looked at Yuichi who was still pulverizing his enamels with the toothbrush. The moan seemed to be coming from the space between the toothbrush now arched upwards and the open mouth of Yuichi. It was startling, but Andrew could see no signs of pain in Yuichi's face, he looked more relaxed really. It took a while, but he finally got it. "Moonriver." Yuichi was moaning the chorus to "Moonriver."

At a stoplight Yuichi turned to Andrew, wet toothbrush in hand, "You work in beef, right?"

"I'm a pot roast consultant," Andrew said.

"Is it interesting?"

"Sometimes" he said trying to conjure up that picture—that goal as the light turned green and Yuichi rolled through the intersection then re-inserted the toothbrush into his mouth. He pulled in front of the apartment building, and Andrew opened his door.

"How much do you get paid?" Yuichi asked abruptly.

"About 200,000 yen a month," Andrew said back too tired to do anything but answer his question."

"Nnn," Yuichi said then reached for his toothbrush.

"*Goschisosema desita,*" said Andrew, thanking him for the food and whiskey then shut the car door.

~

Andrew changed clothes and lay on the tatami mat before the TV in his apartment. From the corner of his eye he could see the fax machine—the nexus between him and his mustached boss sitting in Chicago behind his maple desk adorned with a glass cow paperweight. The tray was empty, but Andrew knew it would soon fill with new instructions, new mercilessly undisguised criticisms, and if matters stayed on pace it wouldn't be long before that mustached boss called him back to Chicago. Andrew would be called back to park in Red Lobster and Ponderosa parking lots to negotiate shit, unchewable beef with fat-ass franchise owners who talked at length about the decision to dispense mint-flavored tooth-picks, *which sure cost a little more but* . . . Andrew groaned out loud and thought about destroying the machine, but opted to turn the television on instead.

The Nagoya Dragons were playing the Tokyo Giants in Japanese baseball. It was 3-3 in the bottom of the ninth with the Dragons at bat, one out and the bases loaded. The Dragons were a working class baseball team, and Andrew grew to like them very much. They were the Japanese White Sox, he figured. The Tokyo Giants were a big money team with endless resources and a brooding Darth Vader-like manager. They were the Japanese Yankees Andrew convinced himself and easily vilified them. A white guy was batting for the Dragons, every team in the league was allowed to import two Americans on their squad. The strike zone is radically smaller than the American one; it's a hitter's game. The white guy had driven the count to 2 balls and no strikes, the perfect hitter's pitch. Everyone watching knew what was next—fastball down the middle. He had to bring it to him, and sure enough he did. The white guy smashed the ball; smashed it right to the short stop who caught it then stepped on second to complete the double play. "Shit." Andrew yelled then got up for the last Kirin in the miniature fridge. He was preparing himself for extra innings. He never left a tied game. Once he sat in the stands of old Commiskey Park for 6 1/2 hours: White Sox vs. Indians 1989—both teams were out of contention, but it didn't matter. Andrew sat down on the tatami ready for the tenth when a Samurai movie came on. He thought it might be an advertisement, but it wasn't. The game was over. *No extra innings, what type a shit?* He hollered at the television cart. Shortly after came a knock at the door—the keep it down knock. Andrew was about to get the keep it down speech in another country, he thought proudly to himself, as he prepared a sleepy face for the opening of the door, which revealed a perfectly coifed young lady erect on black high heels. Maki.

"*Sitzude simasu,*" she said apologizing for appearing at the door. Then removed her heels and walked into the apartment, which displayed a collage of dry cleaning bags, dirty laundry, and various beef paraphernalia.

"You are alone, right?" she asked in English while peering around all three rooms of the apartment stopping at the grand piano in the main room "Oh, you play piano," she asked smiling now with her perfect teeth.

"I can't play. It came with the apartment." Andrew said

"My grandfather bought me a grand piano like this when I was three years old. I can't play well," Maki said, covering her mouth with her hand." My Grandfather bought me the piano because he wanted me to be an elegant lady, Andrew-san," Maki said then pulled the cover to expose the shiny keys.

"What do you think, Andrew-san, am I an elegant lady?"

He told her she was an elegant lady to which she smiled, happy he gave the correct answer.

"So what does Andrew-san think about Yuich-san?"

"Seems like a very interesting person."

"Yes I think so too, and what does Andrew-san think about working for Yuich-san?"

"What?"

"He's very rich."

". . ."

"Yes I know you have a job, but you can work at night for Yuich-san," Maki said then slid her pantyhosed legs in front of the brass piano pedals.

"Two days ago Yuich-san called me. He said you moved in. He spoke fondly of his new American neighbor." Maki paused here, and Andrew's eyes were drawn to her legs, Maki took notice of Andrew's eyes. "He believes there is a definite reason for this, a reason that you moved next door. He believes you are part of his future. He told me this again tonight after speaking with you. He wants your help, and certainly somehow he can help you. He is a rich and wise man."

"What does Yuichi-san do for a living?"

"Men's clothing. He was one of the first in Nagoya with neckties. He owned 140 stores on Honshu not long ago. Now he owns 75, but he has a new idea, and he would like you to help him. He wants to start a business on the Internet."

"I'm very flattered Maki. I really am, but I don't know anything about computers"

"That doesn't matter."

"No?" He replied.

"He believes there is a reason. You should think about his offer. He'll of course pay you a lot of money. He may seem a little crazy, but he is as you say a very interesting person."

"What does he want me to do?"

"I don't want to talk more about this Andrew-san, here is a letter I've translated for you from Yuich-san."

Andrew took the letter from Maki and began to open it when Maki delicately grabbed his wrist and said: "Maybe I could play a song on the piano. Would you like to hear the song before you open that envelope?"

Andrew had no choice, but liked the fact he had no choice. He would love to hear her play, he told her.

"Tonight, be the first *taifu* for you?" Maki asked then began to play an uptempo song on the piano making Andrew wonder if perhaps he were on a game show. This was a wonderful tension for Andrew to feel—the possibility for his conversations to be part of a gameshow. He was thrilled to play along.

"*Taifu*, what's *taifu?*" Andrew asked to which Maki was silent. Instead of asking again he walked to get his dictionary out of the kitchen. *Taifu* he said over and over again. "Typhoon" the dictionary explained. Andrew closed the book angry that he couldn't figure that one out. He thought about what it meant. Typhoon. Tonight. Typhoon. Then walked back to Maki who was playing a song he couldn't name.

"Typhoon tonight?" he asked excitedly to which she again ignored him.

"*Konbon wa Taifu?*" he said louder.

"*Hai.*" She said firmly.

"When? *Nanzi-kara?*"

"*Wakaranai*," (I don't know) she said not looking up from the keys. How will you get home?" he quietly asked, to which she repeated: "*Wakaranai*," in a soft voice, while playing the piano.

Andrew looked through his closet for a robe, sheets and pillow to the sounds of Maki's piano, then turned off the light and laid down to drink his beer. He turned the Samurai movie back on and saw that it was interrupted by a newscast, a cute female newscaster said the word *taifu* with a placid smile. From what Andrew could discern the typhoon wasn't supposed to be fierce, but it stretched from north of Tokyo down to Nagoya, and was expected to hit in the next few hours. He looked outside—the sky was its normal black with shades of blue. The red lights from the television towers still blinked. He laid on the futon holding his beer more than drinking it and listened to Maki play as he fell asleep.

Hours later he woke to the sound of loud wind ripping through the corridor. Maki was awake and bent over him, stretching her hand and wrist next to Andrew's semi-erect penis that somehow snaked its way out of the middle opening of Andrew's boxer shorts. She seemed to be measuring it. Andrew sat up, which startled Maki who smiled nervously then laid back down, her head now four inches from Andrew's.

"It just came out while you were sleeping," Maki said covering her smile with her thin hand. "You had very nice dreams, Andrew-san," Maki said as Andrew snafued his penis back through the boxer hole and stood up. He walked to the fridge for his water jug, and wolfed down two pints of the water in one swallow. Andrew could see the yellow envelope Maki handed him last night on the kitchen table. He also saw a new fax sitting in the tray, but Andrew walked by these things without stopping. The wind was absurdly loud as it cut through the corridor. Andrew looked for his sweatpants then noticed Maki had them on so he walked outside the door in his boxers. It was 4:47 in the morning when he opened the pink apartment door and walked into the wind tunnel. He searched for the mouth of the wind tunnel, where there was an opening for the stairs. He sat in front of them. The sky was yellow and pink and the bamboo forest across the street swayed furiously. Papers blew in fast circles on the street and rain seemed to be falling sideways. No one was outside. Over the wind Andrew could hear chanting from inside the apartment near the stairs, and he could smell with an acute morning nose incense seeping out the bottom of the door. It smelled like pepper and burning wood—it was the same incense used at the Buddhist temples he'd visited in Kyoto. Andrew thought about Kyoto. He walked all day talking only to old ladies at bus stops. Andrew listened to the wind rip through the streets and corridor. While his boxer shorts rippled he looked through the stairwell at the yellows and pinks of the tumultuous Nagoya sky. If he sold no beef he at least had this.

He walked back to his apartment. Maki was asleep or pretending to be. He laid next to her, making sure his freshly measured penis was secure in its confines, then fell back asleep.

YOUR AUNT IS DEAD

Curtis White

Your aunt is dead.

What dead? Dead what?
Your aunt is *dead.*
Whattaya mean dead?
Dead. Dead dead.
Yeah, but what's it.
It's dead.
Dead like . . .
Deader.
Jeezus.
Your aunt is dead.
So you've said.
Dead.
Ok, I get it.
Your aunt is dead.
Will you cut it with that. I told you.
Dead.
Say, how much money do I have?
Your aunt is dead.
And chocolate cake. How much?
Your aunt is dead.
And my penis. It's hard as a rock. Maybe harder.
Dead.
You know what that means?
Dead.
Are you trying to tell me something?
Yes. In fact, I am. I am trying to tell you that your aunt is dead.
Well, how many times you think you got to tell me, already?
Until you get it. Your aunt is dead.
I give up on you. All this talk. Gobbledygook.
It's your aunt. She's dead.
I'm gettin' nowhere with you.
She's dead.
Who do you think you're talking to?
The nephew of your aunt.

Jeezus.

Your aunt is dead.

My dear old auntie?

That's the one.

Which one? The one in the country or the one in the city?

Country.

So, country aunt?

Country aunt.

Country aunt dead?

Country aunt dead.

Tell you what, I'll give you my money and my chocolate cake if you'll just buzz off.

It's your aunt that's buzzed off.

You drive a tough bargain.

Dead.

Oh fuck. A real wheeler-dealer. Killer-diller, too. A regular Mr. Buy-low-sell-high.

Dead.

I know. Jesus Christ, I know. You keep sayin' it. You keep sayin' it and sayin' it. You're drivin' me nuts. Why?

You're implicated.

What? Somebody thinks I offed my dear old country auntie?

Not exactly.

Well, what exactly?

Nothing.

Wait a minute. Feel this.

What?

Feel this. You know what that is?

Dead.

No, you incredible dumb fuck! That's not dead! Man, I'm beginning to think you don't know about death.

Dead to me.

Christ. That's not dead. That's hard. Real hard. That, my friend, is my penis.

Dead.

You are scaring me silly, man. I'm not kidding. Okay, here's my last offer. Money, chocolate cake and the iron-hard penis. Yours. Take them. I don't want 'em anymore.

Don't want 'em.

Don't want 'em!? *You* don't want 'em?

Don't want 'em.

Will somebody tell this guy to shut up? Just shut it! Shut it! It!

Your uncle is dead.

Oh now it's my uncle.

That's right.

Aunt. Uncle. Just like that.

You got it.

Isn't that a bit much? A bit of an unbelievable coincidence?

You think it's a coincidence that both your aunt and uncle died?

What are you laughin' at?

You. You're funny. Your idea of coincidence.

Never mind that. So which one was it? The trombone playin' one or the bicycle ridin' one.

Yep.

Whaddaya mean "yep?" I suppose they're both dead.

Could be.

When the hell did that happen?

Just now.

While we were talkin'? My trombone playin' uncle, husband to my city aunt, died while we were standin' here talkin'? Is that what you're sayin'?

That's right.

That's awful. One right after the fucking other. Like little human dominoes. But how do you know this stuff?

I know.

Yeah, but how?

Just know.

You just know. And why do you keep on staring at me?

I want to know if you have a message.

A message?

Yeah.

What kind of message?

That's up to you.

A message to my dead aunt and uncle? They're dead! That's the point! I can't talk to them anymore! And they didn't even let me know they were sick so I might could have sent them a card.

That would have been nice.

They have some good cards now. Funny, sad, pretty, zany. Card makers nowadays are some clever fucks.

That's nice.

Nice? You makin' fun of me?

Wouldn't do that. I don't need to.

I punched a guy once for that.

What?

Sayin' something smart like that.

I don't need to say anything smart.

Oh, oh yeah. You don't say nothin' smart. Like maybe my wife never says anything smart either. Old Schwartze Tongue.

You call your wife Schwartze Tongue?

Old Schwartze Tongue.

Is that proper?

Hey, I thought you were Mister Don't-Tell-Me-Nothin'-I-Know-It-All-Already? How come you don't know my wife's nickname then?

I never said I know everything. I know what I know.

Well, I'm done with you anyway. I'm takin' a walk.

Don't overdo it.

What? Overdo what? How do you overdo a walk?

Just overdo one and you'll see.

Are there warning signs?

Not that I know of.

Well, what do you suggest I do if you don't think I should be doing the incredifuckably strenuous cardiacal exertion of walking on my two feet?

I thought you'd never ask. Having listened to all the teachers, studied all the sacred texts and tried all the methods, I can suggest the following: you have nothing to rely on, no one to turn to, and nowhere to go. I suggest that you sit solid and unmoving and determined as a mountain, until, finally, after six days your eyes will open on the rising morning star and you will realize that what you have been looking for has never been lost.

What? Are you trying to tell me that I've wasted all this time listening to crapola from some self-made New Age guru? Fuck that shit. I'm gone.

That's right.

Three Letters to the President

Harvey Strub

4651 Hope Valley Road, Apt. J
Durham, NC 27707
June 11, 2001

President George W. Bush
The White House
1600 Pennsylvania Avenue NW
Washington, DC 20500

Dear President Bush,

Last night, while out on my daily walk, I happened upon a brother and sister. I was proceeding north, and they were approaching me from the opposite direction. The sister was perhaps eight and the brother was perhaps ten. They were both dressed for the season. The sister was wiry and energetic. She wore large plastic glasses and had her hair pulled back in two places on the sides of her head. She took big, bounding steps and ran ahead of the brother. When she drew even with me, she turned back and looked at her brother and yelled to him. "Come on, Jefferson," she said. The brother kept walking at more or less the same speed he had been. He did not look up at her. He had a flat-footed way of walking. Jefferson was one of those ten-year-olds whose face and general appearance uncannily prefigure how he will look upon his retirement from a fairly good job with a large insurance company. Until then, until he grows into his face, Jefferson's peers will heap large quantities of abuse upon him, that much is clear.

The sister called out to her brother again. "At this rate we'll never make it home. Kick it, Jefferson."

Jefferson did not reply. As before, he didn't even glance up.

The sister said, "It's almost TV time. Come on."

By this time, roughly fifteen feet separated Jefferson from me. This was when a squirrel darted onto the path. Both Jefferson and I stopped in our tracks and stared at the squirrel between us. The squirrel was the gray kind, and it had a snake caught in its jaws. The snake was one of those thin, green numbers, measuring probably fifteen or sixteen inches in length. The snake hung from either side of its mouth like a Fu Manchu moustache. It twitched and writhed out of leftover nervous energy.

Jefferson said, "Holy shit."

I said, "I know, man."

The squirrel didn't move. Neither Jefferson nor I took a step forward. The squirrel, I could tell, was running through a series of complex calculations, processing everything from the distance to certain shadows to the height and thickness of certain trees.

By now the snake's head hung limp, but its tail still had some life. It twisted up, curling and uncurling. It struck the path and lashed at the squirrel.

Jefferson's sister came up from behind me to see what in the world we were staring at. She made a noise, as if something with many more syllables were caught back in her throat, and then stood as transfixed as her brother and I.

Jefferson said, "Cool."

His sister said, "That's fucking sick."

I said, "This is an image on which the three of us can found our city. Maybe a better Durham, if you want to do it that way. Or else maybe an entirely new city, with a new name. It's up to you guys."

Jefferson and his sister looked at me like I was nuts.

I said, "I'm not nuts."

The sister said, "Whatever."

I said, "The Aztec peoples located their great city of Tenochtitlan (tuh-no-cheat-lahn), or the place of the prickly-pear, at the exact spot where they came upon an eagle devouring a snake while perched atop a cactus."

The sister said, "You are so nuts."

"Listen," I said, "It gets better. Huitzilopochtli (wheat-seal-o-poached-lee), a god of theirs, generally thought to be their god of war, had previously informed this wandering tribe of Aztecs to like be on the look-out for an eagle with a snake in its beak sitting on top of a cactus, and that is precisely what they saw. This was in the year 1325."

Jefferson's sister took a step back and turned to walk away.

I said, "Their god spoke to them then. He said, 'Hey, guys, this here is the place.' All the Aztecs began to cry. They were just so glad to finally see the eagle with the snake in its beak. They were no doubt hungry, and they were no doubt tired. They had been on the road for, like, ever. They were ready to settle down, maybe rest for a couple of days, and then start building shit. Their god sang to them then. He sang, 'This is Mexico! This is Tenochtitlan. This is where the eagle extends its wings and eats snake, where the fish fly out of the water and the serpents whisper! This is Mexico. This is Tenochtitlan. And many great things will happen here.'"

Jefferson's sister called out for her brother to follow. Jefferson looked at me, shrugged, and started to leave. Then he stopped. "You think something like that could happen here?" he asked. He pointed at the ground around his feet. "You think something like that could happen again, like it did before?"

"I don't know," I said. "Maybe. It just seems strange is all." I nodded to the squirrel. The snake was still now. "That's all I'm saying, I guess, it just seems really strange."

Jefferson gave the squirrel a wide berth and moved with a cautiousness that was somewhat surprising to see. That left me with the gray squirrel and the green snake. It was starting to get dark. After maybe a few more minutes, the squirrel ran off with the snake, and I went home.

Keep up the good work, sir.

Sincerely,

Harvey Strub

4651 Hope Valley Road, Apt. J
Durham, NC 27707
June 18, 2001

President George W. Bush
The White House
1600 Pennsylvania Avenue NW
Washington, DC 20500

Dear President Bush,

Back in early January, Nancy and I agreed to help out on a project for Abby's and Nick's daycare. The project was that Abby and Nick and the other kids were going to spend several days learning how to make paper by hand. The daycare is run out of the apartment lived in by Sara Tompkins, who, for reasons I have never quite understood, goes by the name of Joe. Joe is basically this old hippie woman with long gray hair styled in a manner I always thought bore a strong resemblance to a mountain, particularly when she is seen from behind. To give you some idea of the whole timeframe, this would have been just before Nancy's and my separation, in the days when I did things like take Abby and Nick to daycare and when seeing Joe from behind was something that happened every weekday. I held Abby's and Nick's hands, and we walked up the sidewalk like that, and I called out, "Morning, Joe. Harvey here, with Abby and Nick," and Joe, who appreciates a gentle warning like that as she tends to startle easily, she turned and smiled and said, "Morning there, Harvey. Morning there, Abby. Morning there, Nick."

Joe has a way with kids and a whole bunch of ideas for things to do with kids during the day while the adults are away at work. Case in point: making paper by hand. Now the idea was that the adults were going to help out with all this papermaking. Some volunteered to help during their lunch times, while others would help behind-the-scenes, for example with the supplying of some of the supplies the kids needed.

Nancy and I, because we couldn't get off work, were helping in a behind-the-scenes way. What we had to do is we had to collect some old cotton clothes from around the house or from neighbors or relatives, cut those old clothes into bite-sized pieces, and then boil those pieces until we stopped seeing soap bubbles. Joe said you could also use old silk clothes, if you had silk clothes.

The night before all the boiled pieces of cloth were due, Nancy and I stayed up late working. Nancy was out in the breakfast nook, cutting up a t-shirt of mine that read, "Charity Fun Run 10K," the origin of which was something of a large-scale mystery to both of us since I had no recollection whatsoever of participating in any such event.

"I don't remember any Fun Run," I said.

Nancy said, "Maybe your boyfriend Ted gave it to you." Now to give you some background here, Nancy frequently referred to guys I am friends with as my boyfriends. Ted, in this case, is Ted Murkowski, a long-time coworker of mine and all-around great guy.

"Maybe so," I said. I frequently did this thing where I pretended what Nancy said either didn't quite compute in my brain or in any case did not bother me one iota.

Nancy nodded, put her head back down to work, and was soon like a feverish machine again with the scissors on that Fun Run t-shirt.

Meanwhile, back in the kitchen, I was standing in front of the stove, watching four large boiling pots filled with the cut-up remains of my blue jeans. When the water in a pot boiled off, I took it from the stove, carried it to the sink, filled it with water, and put it right back on the burner. I also stirred the blue jean pieces with a wooden spoon. I stirred the pots clockwise and then, when the pieces were really spinning around at a good clip, I stuck my spoon back in and started turning counterclockwise. Then I did the reverse. Then the reverse of the reverse. The stirring was by no means necessary. It was just something I liked to do. It passed the time.

From out in the breakfast nook, Nancy called out, "All done."

"What's that," I said, coming around the corner.

"I'm all done," she said. She pointed with the business end of the scissors at the several variously colored mounds in front of her. We had collected t-shirts, pants that no longer fit me, blouses from when Nancy had an office job, and a set of my father's hankies that my mother gave me when he died.

My mother had been cleaning out my father's dresser, and I was sitting on the edge of their bed, meaning to keep her company. She put some stuff into garbage bags to take to the Salvation Army and presented the rest to me. "Here," she said, "why don't you take these?" She handed me a stack of hankies, all neatly folded and ironed. It wasn't a question really.

"Thanks," I said. "Thanks, mom." I took one hankie off the top and looked at it, turning it over as if I thought it might be different on the bottom, and then put it back into place.

The truth was I never wanted the hankies, and I never used them. To be honest, I never did grasp the point of the hankie. But I kept them. I hung onto them for years. I couldn't just throw something like that out, not that I didn't consider it, often. All of which is to say I was glad to see them cut up. Now the kids could make the finest white paper out of them. Then they could draw all over the paper, glue other pieces of paper to the paper, and hang all those pretty things in the windows, pretty things that I'd come to admire when I picked up Abby and Nick after work, asking them to show me which ones are theirs and then also where is so-and-so's, so-and-so here being the name of some friend.

"My work here is done," Nancy said. She surveyed the length of the table.

"You going to bed?"

"I'm going to bed," Nancy said.

"I get a kiss?"

She blew me a kiss.

By this time the two rear pots were in dire need of water. The pieces of blue jeans were just simmering and hissing away. I filled the pots with water and set them back on the stove.

This is when I went into the den and lay down on the couch. I started reading the newspaper, then I got up for some juice, lay back down, and started in again with the newspaper. Nothing on the front page seemed to outrage me, so I suspect that is right about when I fell asleep.

When I woke up, the apartment was full of the most acrid, blackest smoke I have ever witnessed. The smoke detector was doing its thing, and someone looking like Nancy ran out of the bedroom toward the kids'.

In the kitchen, the smell was like fried hair and burnt plastic mixed in with some brand of chemical unholiness. I shut the burners off. The pot on the right rear burner had flames shooting out, so I pulled it off the stove. I was going to take it to the sink and fill it full of water. I think I had in mind that I'd start them all boiling again. This time I'd do a better job of keeping an eye on the water level. I was, for all purposes and intents, still asleep. I no sooner put water in the bottom of the pot then the bottom of it cracked and fell off. Smoke came up out of the sink and into my face. I gagged, my eyes watered and burned, and I turned away as if in horror or pain.

Next thing I knew the kids were dressed and at the door. They had shoes on and coats over their pajamas. Nancy had her hands on their backs, guiding them forward. They were all three bent over, choking, their hands at their mouths.

"Harvey," Nancy said, "what the fuck are you doing?"

"Cleaning this mess up," I said. I thought it was pretty obvious.

Nancy looked at me as if I was crazy. "I called the fire department," she said. "We're going outside." And then they were gone.

I rushed about throwing open all the windows. I found three fans, plugged those in, and started pointing them in various directions. I got creative and had this big piece of cardboard that I employed to shoo the smoke in the direction of the trio of fans, which in theory then blew the smoke right out the open windows. When the fire department people arrived, in their big boots and coats and those things over their faces, I was standing in the middle of the den, whipping a beach towel around in the air above my head.

The fire department people escorted me out of the apartment and then downstairs, where the ambulance people put drops in my eyes, shined a light down my throat, treated me for smoke inhalation, and released me so long as I promised not to go into the apartment until morning. I promised, and they left. I looked around for Nancy and the kids and didn't see anyone anywhere. The car was gone. I went back upstairs to the apartment and slept out on the porch. It was rough, but it was only for a night. No big deal. Nancy and the kids, I found out later, spent the night at the local Microtel, a chain establishment that offers highly affordable rooms that are a bit smaller than the average motel room.

Nancy has consistently told me that the fire was not the reason she left me. She has told me that the fire and at least nineteen other things I've suggested are not the reason she left me, and I believe her. I believe all twenty things are irrelevant to her leaving, or maybe are minor or just beside the point. I believe her absolutely. From time to time, however, I still think of the fire. I'll be lying here on the carpet, for example, and looking up at the ceiling, when some bit of the smoke smell will get into my nose. That's when I picture myself shielding my eyes with one arm as I rushed about throwing open the windows with the other, and at these times I cannot help but think next of her leaving later.

Keep up the good work, sir.

Sincerely,

Harvey Strub

4651 Hope Valley Road, Apt. J
Durham, NC 27707
June 25, 2001

President George W. Bush
The White House
1600 Pennsylvania Avenue NW
Washington, DC 20500

Dear President Bush,

I just dreamed you and I were brothers. We were roommates, sharing an apartment together. Our place was real nice. It looked a lot like my current apartment, except with furniture. You stayed in what is now, in reality, my bedroom. I camped out on the floor of what is now my computer room and a storage area for empty boxes. I slept on a sleeping bag and one of those foam mattresses.

When I woke up it was broad daylight. You were dressed already and showered. You had your bags packed and by the door. By the looks of things you had been awake and busy for several hours. Your bags included two suitcases that our grandparents had given to us years ago, suitcases that I always considered ours to keep and use together.

There was a pleasant smell all throughout the apartment. Tomatoes and celery and spices. The pleasant smell is what woke me up finally. "What's that smell?" I asked.

"I'm making soup," you said.

And indeed you were making soup. I stood at the counter that divides the kitchen from the breakfast nook and watched as you took the cover off my large pot, cut an orange in half, and squeezed that half of an orange into the soup. You dipped a spoon into the soup, stirred it around a bit, and then you brought the spoon to your mouth. You blew on the soup and then tasted it. I often bring my mouth to the spoon, we're different that way, you and I. Your manners are far superior to mine.

You made a sour face and then turned serious and contemplative once more. Something was missing from your soup, so you squeezed another half of an orange into the pot and stirred. Then you replaced the cover, turned around and asked me what I was looking at.

I was surprised you were leaving. I said, "I'm surprised you're leaving, Mr. President."

"Look," you said, "I have work to do. I'm a busy guy."

I said, "I just always figured you'd stay, that you would, you know, do your work and still continue to live here, that we'd stick together. I always counted on that."

You said, "That's not going to cut it anymore, bro."

I didn't understand why this was happening. I said, "Why is this happening? I don't understand."

I should say here that I believe you were functioning as my older brother in this dream. Clearly, I was carrying on like a younger brother does, even though in life I am an older brother.

You said, "That tells me a whole lot, your not understanding."

"What do you mean?" I asked.

You said, "This is my wake-up call."

"A wake-up call?" I said. "For what?"

You said, "You're sending me a message here, bro, and I'm getting it loud and clear."

"What the hell does that mean?" I asked.

Moments later, when you picked up the two suitcases and somehow or other managed to tuck the pot of soup under your arm, I did not try to stop you. I did not stand in your way or block the door. I did beg you to reconsider your actions, but I did not bar your progress through any physical means.

There was a time when our parents were leaving our grandparents. We were all together as a family, visiting. It was the summer. Our parents had those two suitcases then, and our grandparents didn't want our parents to leave. They were having some fight. It was late, well past midnight. We were leaving suddenly, earlier than we had planned. In desperation, our grandmother grabbed at one of the suitcases, saying that it was her suitcase. I was nine or ten at the time, maybe older but not by much, and I grabbed the suitcase back out of her hands. I said, "No, you gave us that suitcase. That suitcase is ours now." Our grandmother looked stunned, to hear those words and to witness such behavior from me. You can understand why I resolved not to make a big deal out of our suitcases. I didn't want any fuss. I didn't want a scene. So you left then. You took your soup and our suitcases, and you took off.

Keep up the good work, sir.

Sincerely,

Harvey Strub

Project:
Gean Moreno and William Cordova

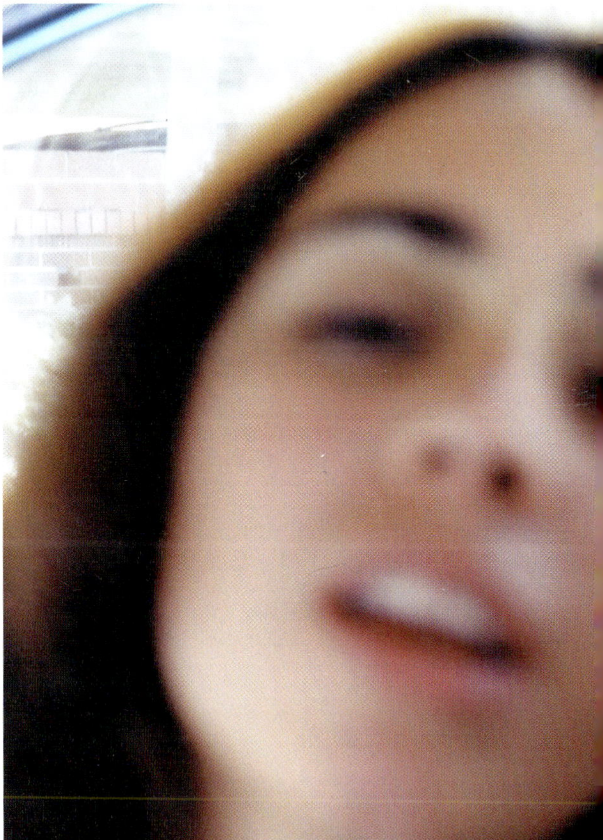

TANS Perú
CUSQUEÑA

Don't you cry (Indianapolis 91)

Don't you cry (II live Joe Robbie 91)

Don't you cry (Demotape 90)

Sentimental movie (DEMO 90)

Waterspouts (cold cuts)

CRASH Diet (DEMO 90)

Nowhere man (Japan 66)

Nowhere man (Munich 66)

Nowhere man (Japan 66 II)

Nowhere man (candle stick park 66)

Nowhere man (ultra rare trax)

Nowhere man (unsurpassed)

Nowhere man (Demo)

like a rolling stone (Berkley 65)

This is My Day (E.P.)

Teddy Boy (69)

Junk (69)

all things must pass (69)

Most of the time (Radio city 89)

lady Marmalade (James L. Knight 92)

Somewhere over the rainbow (James L. Knight 92)

I'm A believer (Flagler 86)

A little bit me, A little bit you (Flagler 86)

King of Rock (Disney 88)

peter piper (Disney 88)

I'm Down (Japan 66)

Miss Fat Booty (live 00)

peanut butter, jelly time (mastmix 01)

peanut butter, jelly time (97.7 create)

Sally, that girl (retro-mix)

Drop The bass (remix 90)

Ballroom dancing (wings rehearsal

Beth (E.P.)

Beth (Demo)

Beth (live rehersal 79)

Beth (unplugged-cut)

Beth (Alt-Mix Audio (studio) (79)

Sarah (video mix)

Sarah (E.P.)

Sarah (Album version)

tell All the people (N.Y.M.S.G. 68)

you were always on my mind (w.n.)

tell all the people (demo 68)

under pressure (D. Bowie vocals only

phat nuts (R.Z.A. outtake) (G

Sweat off my Balls (Maxi-single

candy (E.P.)

still Dre (video version-clean)

November rain (acoustic 90)

INTERVIEW: JEANNE DUNNING

Meredith Goldsmith

What if you could take yourself, and then take yourself outside of yourself, and see yourself as something separate from yourself?" Jeanne Dunning asks. She asks a lot of questions like this lately in her photographs and videos where models ambivalently confront the gooey liquids that cover them, the cumbersome, fleshy masses that (might) overwhelm them, and the artificial skin they put on or leave behind.

It is rare to see such tight integrations of photography and sculpture, and her work consistently, successfully opens up issues of the body, mind, and the borders between that we often keep securely closed.

Dunning exhibits constantly, most recently in Chicago at Bodybuilder and Sportsman Gallery, and fans of her work can look forward to a web-based project she is working on for DIA that opens May 16. I sat down to ask *her* a few things—this woman who reads psychoanalytic theory on her days off, and has as much luck as the rest of us would trying to corral her Labrador when company comes over.

Meredith Goldsmith: Your work has been making me think about how much more familiar we are with our physical selves than our psychological

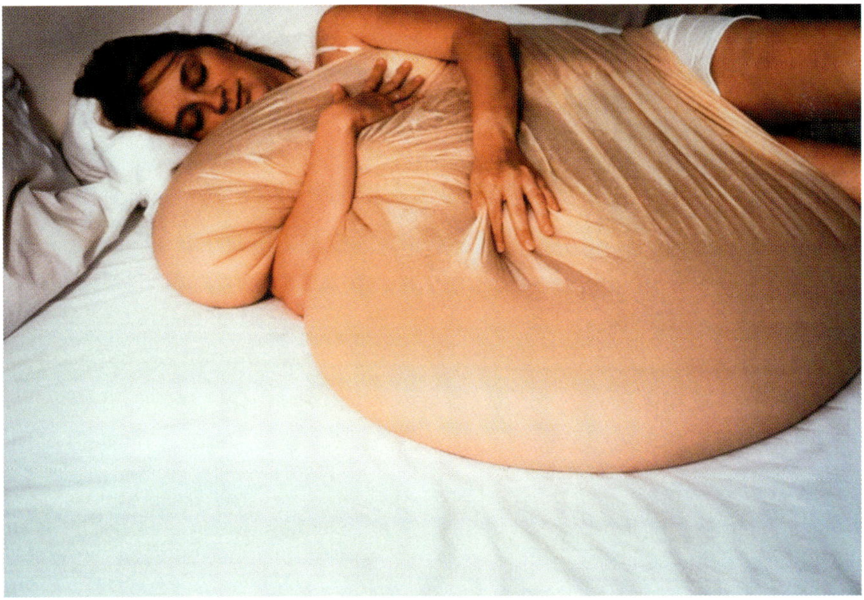

The Blob 3 1999. Ilfochrome mounted to plexiglass and frame 30 1/4 x 41 1/4

selves; particularly how the boundary between our bodies and the world is much more defined than the boundary between the psyche and the outside world. Do you think the difference between those understandings lies in what we can perceive visually?

Jeanne Dunning: Well, I've never thought about it in that way before. Boundaries in general is something I've explored a lot in the work over time, and often it seems to me that we are much more invested in the boundaries and think that they're very clear when they're not. I don't even think the boundary between our physical selves and the rest of the world is as clear as we like to think it is most of the time.

MG: Kind of a default thinking.

JD: Right. And I think, in a way, we are more protective of ourselves when we think that way because it makes us more comfortable to feel like there's a clear boundary between what's us and what's not us. So I've thought about it more in terms of breaking it down, or showing the places where it's much more fragile than we usually think it is. I've never really thought about it in terms of a distinction between what it is literally or physically, and what it is psychologically. The things that my work is about, in terms of our relationship to our own physicality or our relationship to the body, all those physical aspects of it, I always see that as being interesting in and of itself, but also working as a psychological metaphor. So I think I am talking about psychological boundaries and breaking those down as well, and I'm trying to do it with these physical examples. I am definitely thinking of those two things, I just never thought about in one case it being a more clear-cut distinction from the world than another.

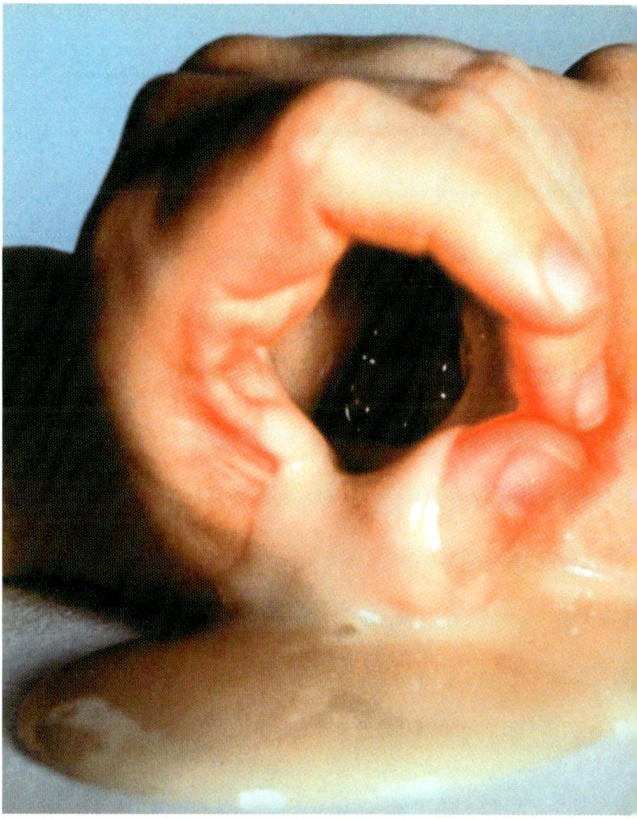

Puddle3 1997. Cibachrome mounted to plexiglass and frame 21 1/2 x 18 3/4

Video Stills, *Trying To See Myself*

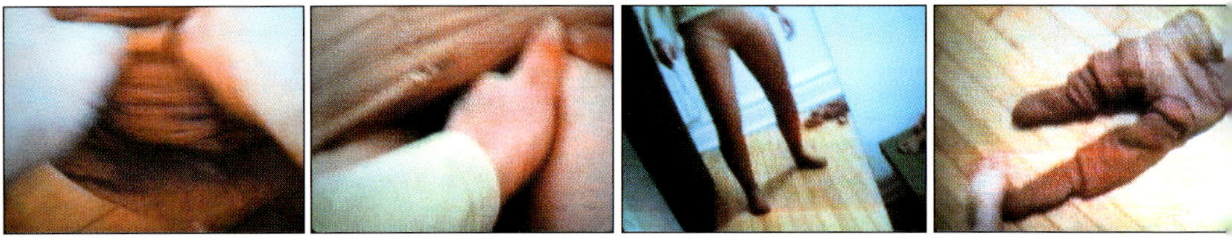

MG: To go back to something you just said in terms of reactions to the work, when I see especially the Blob and Puddle images, it is a very visceral reaction for me and I was just wondering what your relationship is to the work at various stages. If it is still visceral for you initially, and then when does it become more intellectual, for example?

JD: It is still visceral. Of course if almost anybody works with anything for a long time you get a little bit used to it. But I don't feel like those two things are separate I guess, the visceral and the intellectual. I think that in order to get at the ideas in a way that makes them feel real at all, like they mean anything, you need to get that visceral reaction from people, otherwise it can remain abstract.

MG: Right, cause you'd just stay in this heady world . . .

JD: Right, so I don't really separate the two in the way I'm thinking about it when I'm working with it. I see them as both crucial elements that feed off each other, and I don't think the intellectual part is so interesting or would mean very much if you didn't sort of make it grab people.

MG: I'm interested in how you moved from the earlier images which are ambiguous but remain in the interior, and then maybe around 1996, 97, things started to leak, and now your most recent work still deals with ambiguities, but between the interior and the exterior. I'm just wondering how that progression went.

JD: Well there's early work too that depicts exteriors, it's not like it's all interiors, but you're sort of right to pick work from around 96 as a point where I was really specifically thinking in the work about this thing that sort of came up in your first question, this thing about the borders between inside and outside and the distinctions we make between the inside and the outside, or, what's part of us and what's not part of us. And I was specifically thinking in the work about making images that suggest losing that distinction, where suddenly it isn't so clear about what's part of you and what's not part of you. And you start to realize that that boundary can dissolve pretty easily. And by the same token it's not so clear what's inside and what's outside, and that can feel like it gets reversed pretty easily. So one of the things, just as an example of that kind of reversal that I was thinking about in some of that work, is the idea of taking that stuff that is usually, we think of as kind of messy and safely contained on the inside, and having it feel like it gets out, and instead of you containing it, it overwhelms you, and contains you. That fe-

-eling of being lost inside of it maybe. And the loss of control.

MG: That loss of control is such a horrifying idea, yet your models seem so indifferent.

JD: Well, I think that one of the things that makes this stuff interesting is that not only are the boundaries and the distinctions between the inside and the outside not so clear, it is also not so clear how we feel about these things when they happen. And I think not only the ambivalence of our reaction to some of them, but even more the kind of conflicting responses that we have to losing control, to all the things we've been talking about, that's one of the things that's interesting. That's what, to me, points toward the idea that these are things that we have trouble with. Like they're sort of sites for contention for us psychologically as you say, and the fact that we have conflicting responses to them is what shows me that they are. So the models often look kind of dead-pan in their reaction because I don't want them to answer the question for the viewer about how they should respond to it. I want it to seem like it could go either way. Maybe they're comfortable with it, maybe it's an everyday thing, maybe they're horrified and alienated by it. I don't want it to be one way or the other, I want it to be all those ways at once.

MG: Keeping in this line, the settings in the videos and photos, all of the ones I have seen, are interior kinds of shots. And they usually reference a home, like you have some women on linoleum floors. And while the settings do provide a vacuum for what's happening and it does reference a private space, I was wondering also if they are meant to reference a female sphere or a woman's world.

JD: No, I didn't mean them to. Although I can certainly understand. I think that's a change in the work. Really up until this work that was at Bodybuilder which starts at around 1997, all the pictures were taken with backgrounds and in settings that didn't tell you anything . They were non-places, they were nowhere, or everywhere or anywhere. And it was with these pictures that I started to show enough of an environment that you got some sense that it was happening in a particular place.

I think that for this particular work one of the reasons I chose those kinds of spaces is because I also want the work to seem really normal in a certain way. It would be very easy to emphasize the certain surreal elements in it, but what I'm interested in is having people relate to it as something that is sort of familiar, or something like their lives. And then the reason they're sort of domestic spaces, kitchens and bathrooms, and bedrooms, as opposed to public spaces or even living rooms, is because what I was thinking about in that work really has to do very specifically with your relationship to your physical body. And so those are the places where you have to confront yourself physically by yourself, and I think it was partly for that reason.

MG: One of the things that struck me about the video *Trying To See Myself* is how differently I felt about the nylons after you take them off. Before you put them on they are objects, and after you take them off they seem really invested with your self, like a removed extension of you. This happens frequently in your work where you seemed to have solved the problem of needing to remove parts from yourself by manufacturing new parts for yourself.

JD: Well, if for you, watching that tape, the nylons just start out like any other thing in the world, but then by the end you're so strongly connecting them to me and my body, that they almost seem like a part of my body, that suggests again that that borderline isn't so clear, you know? So I think of it more about those kinds of transitions. And with the role the nylons play in that tape, or with the Blob, or with that gooey stuff that covers the model, the way I think about that stuff is trying to take certain aspects of our bodies and our physicality, and see if you can remove that, so you can look at them separate from the body. So it's not so much creating new parts, it's like taking what's already there and making it more visible and separating it from the body enough that you can try and figure out what your relationship to it is.

MG: Can you tell me about the Tom Thumb web-based project you're working on for DIA?

JD: Yeah, I can. Although I don't have a really short simple way to describe it yet, partly because I'm still working on it, but also because it's kind of a convoluted sort of project.

The thing that had initially gotten me interested in Tom Thumb years and years ago, of course, has to do with the fact that Tom is a body part, and he's a phallic body part at that, so I think I was drawn to it initially for that reason. Even in the more recent versions, which are the ones that people usually know which are based on Brothers Grimm, one of the things that happens to Tom is that he's always going in and out of holes throughout the story. And there are all these earlier versions of the story and they focus even more on Tom just going repeatedly in and out of holes, and specifically, in and out of the body. He spends all his time, over and over and over again getting swallowed by different people and animals, so he's always ending up inside stomachs. And then he always gets out in different ways. Sometimes he gets vomited out, sometimes he gets shat out, sometimes the animal gets killed and he's taken out, and then it all happens again.

So I was interested in that immediately, because of this going in and out all the time, and he's both a person and a body part, and that he keeps going inside the body and coming out again.

But the other thing that I got really interested in, that made me keep pursuing this, is that I realized as I was reading these stories is that there are some really weird parallels I think between Tom's story and the stages that psychoanalysis thinks that infants go through as they mature. You have the oral stage and the anal stage and the phallic phase, and then with Tom, of course, there's all this repetition compulsion because he does it over and over again and keeps being reborn and doing it again. And then you get to the Oedipus Complex. So there are things in the story that really strongly connect to those stages and I thought that was really interesting.

So I'm using the Tom Thumb story, but the other thing, as I kept doing research and thinking about it, I started connecting it with other things that I knew about that shared elements with it. So, just to give you an example, there's a true story of a boy whose last name is not recorded, he's just known historically as Tom. When he was a child he drank some scalding hot soup and it burned his throat so badly that his throat closed up. He couldn't eat. He could breathe, but his esophagus was closed so he couldn't swallow anything. The doctors knew he was going to starve, so they made an artificial hole through his chest leading directly to his stomach, and he fed himself through this hole for the rest of his life, and he lived to be quite old. And then when doctors heard about his condition, they convinced him to let them do experiments putting things in his stomach to learn how digestion worked. The doctors that did these experiments were named doctor "Wolff" with two f's and doctor "Wolf" with one f, and wolves figure in the Brothers Grimm version of Tom Thumb. So here we have Tom, stomachs, swallowing, Wolves, so many elements of the Tom Thumb story.

I have a number of true stories, historical things like this, that share elements with the Tom Thumb story, and what I'm planning on doing with the site is telling all the stories in a parallel way that allows you, through the Internet, to jump back and forth between them at the points of the shared elements.

The other reason I think it will be interesting is that I didn't make anything up. It's all real research that I did. So we have all this stuff that doesn't sound plausible, but actually is true. And I think that people, when they visit art, are going to wonder if it's true or not. Also the Tom Thumb story is a fairytale, so even though all the research I did is real, in theory it never happened. But all these other stories are things that actually did happen. So there's this kind of confusion of reality going on that I think will be interesting.

MG: And the images, are those going to be ones that you create?

JD: I'm creating the images that you'll click on that will let you move from one story to another. I have a picture of the hole in Tom's stomach, and I have all these illustrations from the Tom Thumb books. So I have pictures that illustrate the different stories that are all different kinds of pictures from each other and they're all weird. So I think it will be fun for that reason, too.

Bloodshot delivers Peace and Death for 2002

BOTTLE ROCKETS 'Songs of Sahm'

One of the greatest working bands out there raise their own bad-ass freak flag and kick out the grooves. A raucous and reverent love letter to the great Doug Sahm – the late Texas redneck hippie punk priest. BS 086 $15

PINE VALLEY COSMONAUTS 'The Executioner's Last Songs'

All-star band consigns songs of murder, mob law and cruel, cruel punishment to the realm of myth, memory, and history – all to benefit anti-death penalty causes. Guest singers include STEVE EARLE, NEKO CASE, KELLY HOGAN, EDITH FROST, members of FREAKWATER and THE HANDSOME FAMILY, SALLY TIMMS, and JON LANGFORD. A harrowing record for harrowing times. BS 074 $14

ALSO AVAILABLE:

KELLY HOGAN, ROBBIE FULKS, RYAN ADAMS, NEAL POLLACK, WAYNE HANCOCK, THE YAYHOOS and more.

Write us for a free catalog or check in to **www.bloodshotrecords.com**

BLOODSHOT RECORDS

BLOODSHOT LTD. 3039 W. Irving Park Rd., Chicago, IL 60618

a unique
flower market

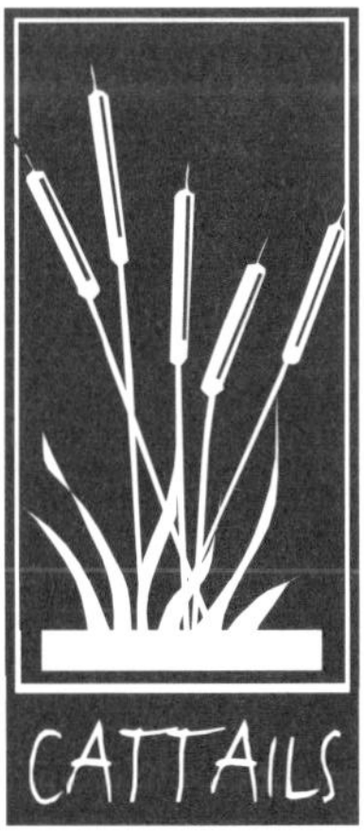

1935 west division chicago
p 773.486.1621 f 773.486.1637

BLUEBLOOD
Blue Collar
a show exploring connotations of blue
curated by meg duguid + maire kennedy
heaven
www.bluebloodbluecollar.org

Art After Humanity

Kevin Blasko

In the April 2000 issue of *Wired* magazine, the essay,[1] "Why the Future Doesn't Need Us" by Bill Joy,[2] considered the end of humanity as we know it. According to the article humanity is rather close to achieving its own demise. The essay specifically discusses the extinction of humanity through the creation of an artificial intelligence that can replicate itself (yes, robots). Mr. Joy's argument is an argument of evolution. If it is reasonably likely that an artificial intelligence superior to human intelligence is created within the next 50 years,[3] then by our own well-documented evolutionary laws, the human race will eventually become extinct – the superior artificial "species" will replicate itself, crowding out humanity and our needed resources (food, water, etc.) to the point where humans could no longer survive. The evolution of machines and the extinction of humanity is the subject of George Dyson's book, *Darwin Among the Machines*[4], who Bill Joy quotes (and I will as well): "In the game of life and evolution there are three players at the table: human beings, nature, and machines. I am firmly on the side of nature. But nature, I suspect, is on the side of the machines."

To be fair, many of the technological advances discussed in the *Wired* article could enhance human productivity and quality of life significantly. Bill Joy pays particular attention to advances in "nanotechnology," that is, technological advances at a scale smaller than the microchip. Researchers are working to develop molecular-level electronics that could reap benefits in agriculture, consumer electronics (you thought they have thin laptops now), and communications. There is also the possibility of molecular level machines called "assemblers" that could build things

TODAY'S MOST COMPLEX VISUAL WORK IS BEING DONE BY PROGRAMMERS, WEB DEVELOPERS, AND "CODE MONKEYS."

and carry out basic instructions, as well as replicate themselves. Advanced technology, such as assemblers, could cure cancer, or if things went terribly wrong, create a variety of genetically superior crab grass that wipes out the planet's edible food, starving out humanity. As the article points out, a product of advanced technology, especially bio-technology, need not be useful (or intelligent) to be superior in the evolutionary sense.

Bill Joy likens the unrestricted growth of powerful technologies to the problems and ethical dilemmas associated with the use of nuclear technologies:

> The nuclear...technologies used in 20th-century weapons of mass destruction were and are largely military, developed in government laboratories. In sharp contrast, the 21st-century technologies – genetics, nanotechnology, and robotics – have clear commercial uses and are being developed almost exclusively by corporate enterprises...building nuclear weapons required, at least for a time, access to both rare - indeed, effectively unavailable - raw materials and highly protected information...The 21st-century technologies...are so powerful that they can spawn whole new classes of accidents and abuses. Most dangerously, for the first time, these accidents and abuses are widely within the reach of individuals or small groups. They will not require large facilities or rare raw materials. Knowledge alone will enable the use of them.

If you believe *Wired*, we have 30 years to figure out what technology means to humanity. The essay could be viewed as a warning bell to a global society that in many respects, is at the total mercy of the technology it has created or the essay could be utterly ignored as apocalyptic drivel. It is my suspicion, though, that this discussion of humanity's relationship with intelligent machines will broaden in the coming years to include intellectual groups that presently may not give a hoot about artificial intelligence. As they always have, artists play a key role in how society examines itself, and it is no doubt that artists will be critical to how this issue unfolds in the public arena. In this particular case, though, artists perhaps have a more prominent role in this discussion than at first it might seem.

Perhaps today's best visual artists do not engage in the world of galleries, museums, and MFA programs. Today's most complex visual work is being done by programmers, web developers, and "code monkeys." They are the silent hands behind software, manipulating code to produce complex and dizzying visual results, whether the end product be a spreadsheet, a web page, or something not immediately useful or aesthetic at all. Today's technological artists, like many contemporary artists, are working with extremely abstract elements, processes, and symbols to develop visual representations for public distribution. Programmers are pushing the intellectual limits more than any other broad group of artists – if you believe Bill Joy, they are in fact slowly, step-by-step, creating an intelligence that rivals our own. Commenting on his own programming work, Bill Joy wrote, "I have never had the feeling that I was designing an intelligent machine. But now, with the prospect of human-level computing power in about 30 years, a new idea suggests itself: that I may be working to create tools which will enable the construction of the technology that may replace our species. How do I feel about this? Very uncomfortable." Today's programmers, perhaps unwittingly, provide through their visual creations some of the most compelling conceptual art available.

Today's software, like other visual implementations, has the ability to be useful and/or beautiful, or neither one. There is a paradox – the struggle of visually representing the abstract code, coupled with the absolute need to do so to engage the public in some form of discourse – that programmers and coders are deliberate in their visual creations. Technically, the code does not have to be visually implemented to be understood (it can be read like text), nor does the code ever have to be executed to be interesting; but just as any conceptual artist, most coders strive to eventually create some visual representation of the code. Even if this final visual representation is 90% driven by the economic need to produce a useful product and 10% motivated by the urge to provide something of aesthetic value, the visual representation of today's software is nonetheless art, in the broadest, postmodern sense of the word.

Software and coding artists produce an interesting postmodern challenge. As the pervasiveness of code-based visual implementations grows and the machine intelligence the code contributes to begins to lapse that of its human creators, we will perhaps find ourselves at a fulcrum in postmodernism. In Lyotard's interpretation, postmodernism is the challenge and deconstruction of the "grand narratives" or "metanarratives" that legitimize the enlightenment and modernist concepts of knowledge.[5] What becomes of postmodernism when the ultimate grand narrative, the infallibility and totality of human intelligence, is annihilated by the birth of an intellectually superior machine? The entire history of humanity is built on the unquestioned superiority of human intelligence second only to God (and of course there are those who argue God is a creation of our intelligence as well). When human intelligence no longer rules, it will be in many ways a great pinnacle for postmodernism – the end of humanity's oldest, enlightenment-era hierarchy.

These developments will also mark a profound shift in terms of art, as we have a human-created intelligent entity – a piece of art if you will – that overshadows its creators. Suddenly, after many years of desanctifying the art object, the object becomes intelligent and begins to "speak," perhaps in words and actions that outshine the artists who created it. The earliest beginnings of this intelligence already permeate every aspect of our culture in a visual manner. Some of the most publicly respected and lucrative creative ventures deal with technology-based media – Internet-based "new media," television, film, video games, and Pokémon. We are a society that marvels and applauds at the leaps and bounds of our software-based media. We love the Internet, Napster, and Hotmail. We think Microsoft is "bad" and support Netscape as some sort of a cultural "hero." More recently, artists have taken to Napster, and discuss it utilizing the lexicon and symbolism of "hero" against a corporate "evil empire." We talk about the visual representation of thousands of line of code as political, ethical, and aesthetic entities under the assumption that the interpretations of meaning for these creations is dictated by humanity (any human, really), not the work itself. We accept the growing intelligence of technology because it's casually assumed to be under our control, but perhaps the control is slowly eroding.

IT IS JUST UNDERSTOOD THAT SUMMER RERUNS OF THE "THE WEST WING" WILL HAVE A GREATER IMPACT ON OUR POSITION ON, LET'S SAY, CAPITAL PUNISHMENT THAN ANY ARTWORK

I wonder if the discourse of our software-based culture is *solely* predicated upon the general understanding that the technology is under humanity's control. If that is indeed the case, if technology evolves over the next several decades and humanity's creations suddenly have a voice on the issues of ethics, meaning, truth, and art, the human assessment of each of those ideas will dramatically shift as the preconditions by which those arenas of discourse exist will have changed or will not exist at all. If the discourse is not grounded firmly on humanity's total control over technology, and we do in fact allow technology a certain stake in the basic human philosophical struggles, then it is significant that we have already conceded major intellectual real estate to machines, our society's increasingly intelligent and complex artwork.

Does the technology we rely on have any more claim to understanding truth and meaning than we do? Certainly no, the command of knowledge does not engender truth or meaning in the human experience, but it does enhance power, which humans have shown can have a great effect on how truth and meaning (and art) are perceived. To consider that a machine, just another piece of art if you will, could have a voice (power) at all is something very different. Is art approaching the age where art will consider itself *and* consider humanity (intelligently)? If you believe Bill Joy, it is fair to say, "With every passing day, art will need humanity a little less."

Michelle Grabner was recently asked whether she thought art is becoming more or less engaged from issues of existence within society. She responded:

> Most young artists seem to have a healthy understanding that art is not an effective vehicle to engage in political change. That is not to say contemporary art does not reflect

> political ideologies. It is just understood that summer reruns of "The West Wing" will have a greater impact on our position on, let's say, capital punishment then any artwork.[6]

The visual work coders produce today contributes, albeit slowly, to a massive shift in human politics over the next several decades as their creations' intelligence increases and perhaps makes decisions on its own. The fact that programmers' art work is not generally abundant in the realm of openings, graduate-school critiques, and other hierarchical systems of art, does not mean that their work is artistically or politically impotent. Michelle Grabner's statement is mostly accurate, however she excludes the growing artistic contributions of programmers and mass media producers. Those summer reruns of "The West Wing" perhaps increasingly constitute "our position", especially in the particular postmodern scenario I am discussing here. "The West Wing" is at the minimum of analysis a basic visual representation of a political ideal communicated through technology. While the technology used to deliver the message is far from "intelligent," it is unlikely to remain so for long – it is the natural evolution of the device to become more complex and intelligent. "The West Wing" exploits the general populace's willingness to accept and embrace political ideas manifested visually through technology.[7] Under the scenario outlined by Mr. Joy, this would perhaps be an important (if not disturbing) foundation for later technology-centered political persuasions.

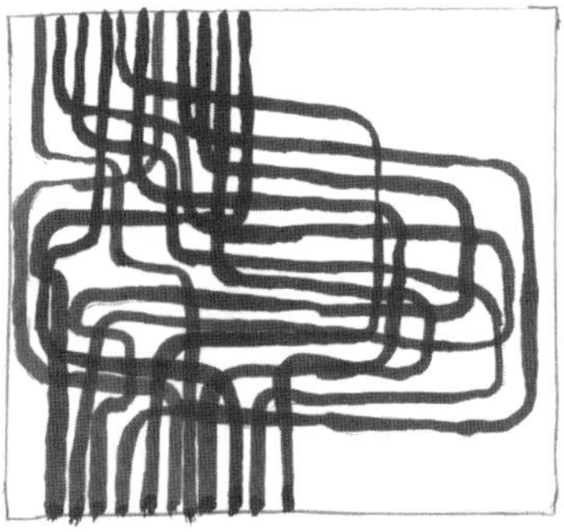

Whether we embrace or reject the future Bill Joy outlines, the unrestricted pursuit of scientific knowledge, fortunately or unfortunately, will surely continue – as scientists, programmers, and theorists develop technologies that will contribute to an eventual free-thinking, artificially intelligent entity. Mr. Joy in his essay thinks the future does not necessarily have to be the future of machine intelligence, calling upon our collective spirit to, "Choose between the pursuit of unrestricted and undirected growth through...technology and the clear accompanying dangers." However, he also asks for the discussion to continue, inviting, "people with many different backgrounds, in settings not predisposed to fear or favor technology for its own sake."

Artists will have a unique opportunity to contribute to this discussion, a discussion that will certainly grow over the years, both in magnitude and its implications. Artists are in fact contributing to it already. Two exhibitions that deal directly with art in the digital age were recently at The Whitney and the San Francisco MOMA.[8] While exhibitions like these and other work that deals with these issues may not force a political movement against technology (if such a movement is even desirable), the exchange of ideas through art, writing, and speech is no doubt humanity's greatest contribution to history and to the future. Artists already have a keen understanding of the deconstruction of hierarchies, especially visual ones, and have much to offer the discussion on humanity's tense relationship to technology. As with many human pursuits, it will be the discourse, not the results of discourse, from which we will gain the most understanding.

---

[1] The article is available online at: http://www.wired.com/wired/archive/8.04/joy.html

[2] Bill Joy is the cofounder and Chief Scientist for Sun Microsystems, one of the preeminent technology companies of our day (and a major rival to Microsoft). He is also the former cochair of a presidential commission on the future of information technology research.

[3] The article cites 2030 as the year when an artificial intelligence more powerful than human intelligence would be feasible.

[4] George B. Dyson. *Darwin Among the Machines: The Evolution of Global Intelligence*. Helix Books,1998.

[5] Jean-François Lyotard. *The Postmodern Condition: A Report on Knowledge*. University of Minnesota Press, Minneapolis, 1984.

[6] From *CakeWalk* Magazine — http://www.cakewalkmag.com

[7] Note an interesting article in Salon.com analyzing the U.S. President character portrayed on "The West Wing" as if he were an actual presidential candidate this election season: http://www.salon.com/ent/col/mill/2000/10/18/west_wing/index.html

[8] More information on these shows can be found at the museums' web sites: The Whitney: "BitStreams: Art in the Digital Age," March 23, 2001 through June 10, 2001 at http://www.whitney.org; SFMOMA: "010101: Art in Technological Times," January 1, 2001(online)/March 2, 2001(galleries) - July 8, 2001 at: http://www.sfmoma.org.

HYDE BROTHERS, BOOKSELLERS

Here to find fine and here-to-fore hard to find BOOKS

www.hydebros.com
(800) 264-6369
1428 Wells Street
FORT WAYNE, INDIANA

FC2

Spring 2002

Harold Jaffe
False Positive

C. W. Cannon
Soul Resin

Marianne Hauser
Shootout with Father

http://fc2.org

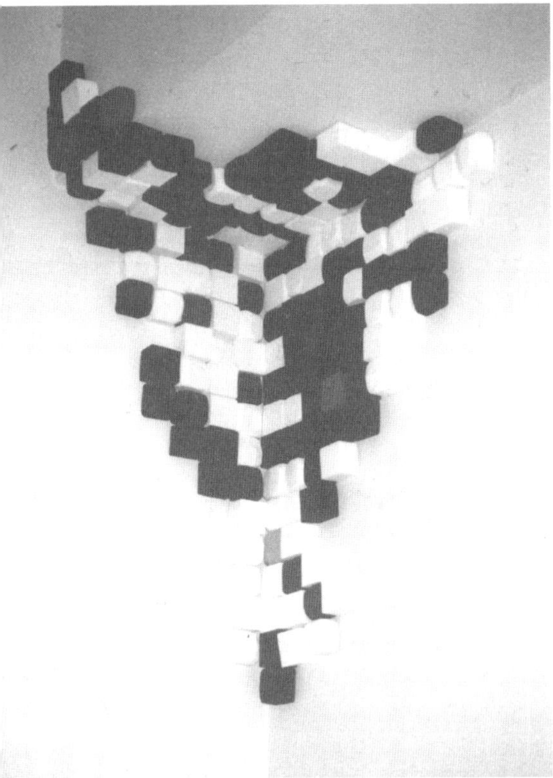

Roadkill

a show by recent graduates of the MFA department at The School of the Art Institute's painting program

Opening reception
Friday May 10th 7-12am
through June 2nd

heaven
1550 N. Milwaukee, 2nd Floor
Chicago, Illinois 60622
heavengallery.com
773-342-4597
hours: Sat. and Sun. 1-5pm

"untitled" by Lisa Caccioppoli 2001 latex paint on 3"X3" carved styrofoam cubes

Powell's Bookstores

We are Chicago's Largest Used Book Dealer, specializing in quality used and out of print books in all academic and scholarly fields. We also have more fiction, poetry, art, and photography than any chain store (and at much cheaper prices).

Three locations in the City:
1501 E. 57th Street 773-955-7780
828 S. Wabash Ave. 312-341-0748
2850 N. Lincoln Ave. 773-248-1444

A STATE OF HYPOXIA

Jan Estep

Hypoxia: an abnormal condition resulting from a decrease in the oxygen supplied to or utilized by body tissue.

Platonic: idealistic, visionary, or impractical.

You focus on taking one more step, lifting your knee, swinging the foot forward, pushing it down into the snow, shifting your weight, and pausing to breathe. For hours your activity has been reduced to this: stepping, breathing, stepping, breathing. With each move your heart pounds so fast and hard it's deafening. It's so loud you picture the muscle filling up and contracting, again and again, forcing blood to your extremities at a ridiculous rate. Each pause you wait for your body to calm itself and are amazed that a simple step forward can cause so much internal disturbance. You step again and wait. When you breathe the cold air rasps against your throat, never seeming to reach your lungs. You draw deeper against the thin air but you're slowly suffocating. The pressure is too low outside the body, getting lower as you move higher. You step again and breathe, all feeling shunted to your weakened limbs. Preoccupied with the effort, you forget what you wanted, why you're here, what the larger goal of this picture is. You wonder if you'll reach the top, whether you'll be aware of yourself when you do, or astonished that there is an end at all.

If someone from sea level were immediately taken to the top of Mount Everest at 29,028 feet, he or she would be unconscious within seconds and dead within minutes. Humans are not meant to survive in extreme altitudes—the highest permanent residents live at 17,000 feet in the Andes and 16,000 feet in Nepal—but given enough time, the body can adapt with a number of physiological changes that allow a person to exist, if not thrive, at high altitudes. The problem lies in the low barometric pressure; relatively speaking there is less oxygen in the air the higher you go, and less oxygen means less fuel for your muscles and brain. The simplest and most immediate way of

YOU LITERALLY BEGIN TO DESTROY YOURSELF IN ORDER TO GO HIGHER ON THE MOUNTAIN. IMMEDIATE DESCENT IS NECESSARY TO STAVE OFF COLLAPSE, UNCONSCIOUSNESS, AND DEATH.

getting the body what it needs is to increase breathing and heart rates. The kidneys then begin to pass more urine trying to secrete the excess carbon dioxide caused by hyperventilating; this diuresis concentrates the blood fluid for richer oxygen transport. The kidneys also release the hormone erythropoietin or EPO, a common but banned blood-doping substance in athletics; EPO stimulates the bone marrow to produce more red blood cells and hemoglobin, further thickening the blood. Myoglobin, which binds with oxygen in the blood, increases, allowing us to take up more oxygen with each breath, and capillaries grow, branching out to bring blood closer to tissue cells.

AT THE TOP OF THE WORLD THE EXPOSURE IS TOO RISKY, THE PERCH TOO DANGEROUS, AND THE DROP-OFFS ARE THOUSANDS OF FEET DEEP. SEEKING SUCH KNOWLEDGE BECOMES PERILOUS.

Along with these positive adaptations, the body begins to compromise its own integrity in order to conserve energy. It starts shutting down, decreasing blood flow to nonessential parts. Climbers become anorexic and can't absorb food, cannibalizing their own muscle mass. They lose fine motor coordination, and the ability to concentrate. As senses are blunted climbers become confused, even hallucinate. Because of the stressed gaseous exchange of oxygen and carbon dioxide, fluid begins to leak into the alveoli and other intercellular gaps; the lungs fill with fluid and the brain begins to press against the skull. Most climbers endure chronic headaches and disrupted sleep the entire time they are on the mountain.

Past a certain point at 20,000 feet acclimatization no longer offsets the body's decline. You literally begin to destroy yourself in order to go higher on the mountain. Immediate descent is necessary to stave off collapse, unconsciousness, and death.

The toll on the body that occurs when mountaineers summit high-altitude peaks such as Everest is remarkable; the structural transformation they undergo is a testament to our ability to adapt to hostile environments. However, in most popular accounts of expeditions, such physiological changes are underplayed. We tend not to hear about the intense discomfort and disorientation, or the brute force required to will oneself up the mountain. No one imagines that the dominant experience on the mountain comprises the simple act of stepping one foot

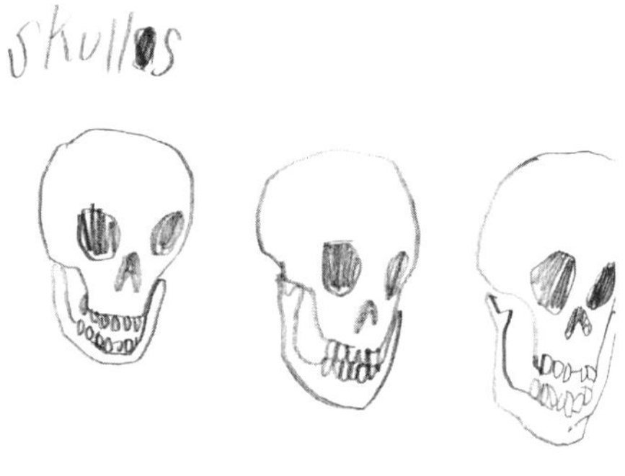

in front of the other, a sheer act of stubbornness and masochistic perseverance. Mythically mountaineering is considered a heroic endeavor, symbolic of man's conquest of nature, and a manifestation of our search for the sublime. Going where no one has gone before, going higher than formerly thought conceivable, seeking the purity of an unparalleled vantage point. The romantic image of the mountaineer is like the ancient yogi a person who seeks transcendence, not someone who is ambitious beyond sensibility, or driven beyond practicality. The mountain represents the unattainable ideal that only a few brave souls believe is within reach.

> I climb the road to Cold Mountain,
> The road to Cold Mountain that never ends.
> . . .
> Who can break from the snares of the world
> And sit with me among the white clouds?
>
> —Han-Shan

In Plato's world the righteous soul rises to heaven to see the eternal forms clearly and purely, a heightened perception that is undistracted by the daily demands of one's ordinary existence, befuddled as that is with shadowy images and ever-changing matter. Plato describes a vertical ontology of more and less real things and then encourages upward movement along an epistemological ladder that takes us from unquestioned opinion to general understanding and finally to certain knowledge. This rational progression is also a move toward brightness and light. As we rise to meet the sun our soul moves away from the false, illusory darkness of the subterranean cave toward goodness and truth. Ascent offers moral and intellectual salvation.

The parallel with mountain climbing is clear: With all the promise of a transformative event mountaineering rewards a climber with progressive knowledge and spiritual release. The high peaks are launching pads to a better life. We just need the constitutional fortitude to pursue the painful dialectical path.

This connection between seeking knowledge and high-altitude trekking is readily apparent in our ordinary language: "to see" or "to see clearly" means to understand; to have "far-reaching vision" entails an appreciation for complexity; we say "higher education" and "higher knowledge"; we learn in "steps"; we feel ourselves on "the edge of an abyss" or "on slippery footing" when we do *not* understand. Yet on the highest mountains, the higher a person climbs, the dumber he or she gets. Devastated by the means the climbing makes one physically and emotionally unable to recognize the ends. Hypoxia triggers a cascade of cognitive and physiological failures. The diminishing air pressure obstructs our breathing, the brain struggles to make sense and stay focused, the body fights against its own deterioration, there is severe danger of pulmonary edema and cerebral swelling. In most cases, as a climber moves to the summit awe and exhaustion render him or her incapable of exercising good judgment. Plus, the higher one goes, the windier, colder, steeper, and icier it gets. At the top of the world the exposure is too risky, the perch too dangerous, and the drop-offs are thousands of feet deep. Seeking such knowledge becomes perilous.

Furthermore, it takes so much time and effort to reach the summit, with an equal effort required to come safely down, that a climber cannot remain at the top for very long. One wants to rest after the arduous ascent, to contemplate the extraordinary circumstance, but the longer you linger, the more you are vulnerable to the effects of starvation, dehydration, suffocation, and hypothermia. All that work and persistence allow only a brief moment of contemplation. As tempting as it may be, even Plato's philosophers cannot remain long in the lofty world of ideas.

WHEN WE SEEK SOMETHING THAT IS SO DIALECTICALLY OTHER TO SENSIBILITY, WITHOUT EMPIRICAL REFERENCE, WE LOSE TRACK OF WHAT COMPRISES WISDOM, WHAT GREATER MEANING THE CLIMB REVEALS.

If we pursue the paradoxical nature of high-altitude ascents—that a person becomes less and less capable of appreciating the summit the closer he or she gets to it—and relate this to the search for knowledge, then something similar happens when a person tries to conceptualize an extremely abstract idea. When questioning the meaning of a metaphysical concept like "freedom" or "beauty," the closer one comes to grasping the truth, the harder it is to focus. Discriminations of meaning become more difficult to entertain the more ethereal and materially ungrounded they are. Do we really know what "the sublime" means? Isn't the sublime precisely that which is beyond our ability to know clearly and distinctly? It's like trying to make the invisible visible or the infinite comprehensible—or trying to make the gods speak in language humans understand. Mystics and mathematicians alike have gone mad in the quest. We wrap our minds around a particular concept and struggle to externalize an internal process, but we verge on nonsense with every step we take. At a certain point, knowledge becomes metaphysically impossible. We have these words and ideas, we use them trying to locate ourselves and clarify what we (think we) mean, and yet we are confronted with the Socratic conundrum of

looking for something we do not know, and possibly cannot know: How will we recognize it when we see it? Are there criteria we can count on? When we seek something that is so dialectically other to sensibility, without empirical reference, we lose track of what comprises wisdom, what greater meaning the climb reveals. And yet such is the life of the mind that it repeatedly takes us to places that are unfamiliar and opaque, always just out of reach, pulling us ever upward but with delirious, haphazard results.

Trekking the high roads, we are always in jeopardy of contracting mountain sickness. Certain adaptations can be made preparing us for the impact of the climb: repeated exposure to abstract thinking acclimatizes a person to the feeling of ungroundedness and to the process of stepping forward and upward despite resistance and uncertainty. We get used to the internal disturbance and confusion. We grow accustomed to the unsure footing. Yet, despite our desire to know and to see from the top of the mountain, the way is riddled with paradox, and at a certain point descent becomes mandatory.

A man spends his whole life dedicated to discovering the meaning of what is good, beautiful, and true. He spends his days walking the high peaks of the Himalayas, the Alps, and the Rockies, conditioning his body to live at higher and higher altitudes. On his best days he takes three good steps, one in the morning, one in the afternoon, and the last after the sun has gone down. It is this last step in the coldest, darkest night of which he is most proud, believing that this bravery will be rewarded best.

One day he sees another man climbing the mountain whose actions appear casual, calm, and unconcerned. Surprised, the man questions the fellow traveler about the seeming ease with which he moves. "I have fallen many times off these peaks, and many times I have survived. I will certainly fall again."

On another day the man runs into a yak, laden with heavy packs lumbering up the mountain. The animal moves slowly but consistently, pushing his front legs ahead of him and digging a path in the snow. The man watches the yak swaying from side to side, head down to the ground, a resolute mass of conviction and instinct. The man watches as the yak is almost buried in the deepening snow, his hooves slipping on the increasing pitch, yet the animal moves forward at a steady, methodical pace. "I was born on the mountain. I live on the mountain. This is what I do."

All in all the man's progress is good, buoyed by the course of his fellow travelers. But on the lowest, loneliest days, when hesitation and doubt rule his thinking, and when confusion clouds his vision, the man pauses to rest, wondering if one more step is possible.

In the back of it all is the mountain, silently, indifferently waiting to be climbed.

Art Chicago 2002

May 10–13 at Navy Pier

Celebrating Ten Years

For more information contact: **Thomas Blackman Associates,** 230 West Huron, Chicago, IL 60610,

Tel 312.587.3300, Fax 312.587.3304,

info@artchicago.com or visit **www.artchicago.com**

chicago's online arts magazine presents its sophomore issue:
"Peaks and Valleys, In Search of the Miraculous"

www.k-d-p.com features interviews with the NFA Space and Jeff Tweedy from Wilco, plus original prose, art reviews, music reviews, and much much more...

KDP presents the much anticipated video art subscription

to order your copy of RESULT (one: $27 / year: $75) e-mail us at adoration@k-d-p.com or send your check or money order (payable to k-d-p) to:
K-D-P 1658 N. Milwaukee Ave. #320 Chicago, IL 60647

EXCALIBUR

"Spring Forward"
A Group exhibition curated by Marty Lazer

May 24-August 16 2002
Opening reception: Friday May 25, 5-10 p.m.
Participating Artists:
Sue Gustafson
Marge Korschgen
Lisa Ruth
Cathy Sorich

Artist-in-residence: Bobberate Monley

VISION
640 North Dearborn Street
Chicago, Illinois 60610
312.266.1944

april - june
The Pond with MICHELLE GRABNER & BRAD KILLAM

july - august
The Pond

The Pond

1152a north milwaukee
thepondproject@hotmail.com

PHENO-MEME-OLOGY OF THE CELLPH:

AN ANALYSIS OF EVOLUTION THROUGH THE HABITUAL USE OF A TECHNOLOGICAL APPENDAGE

M.D. Tschaepe

Within contemporary society a new form of self has arisen due to evolution, yet this new form of self is not the result of genetic evolution. Rather, the new form of self is the result of technological evolution, and just as Richard Dawkins had postulated a theory of memetics that accounted for cultural evolution, we must now account for a more specialized force within human evolution: the technological meme, which I will deem the *t-meme*.[1] The t-meme differs from the standard cultural meme, for it accounts not only for a cultural belief system or practice,[2] but the literal adoption of new technological appendages that become part of the body and its practices. One of the most powerful t-memes within recent evolution has been the cellular phone, and with the advent of cellular technology many human beings have evolved from the 'self' into the '*cellph*'. My purpose within this essay is to explore what this new form of self entails, i.e., what it means to be a 'cellph'.

In exploring this evolved cellph, we must first investigate the self from which it came. First, the self, following the thought of Merleau-Ponty, is an experience inhabiting the world.[3] We must protect ourselves from falling into the Cartesian theater in reflecting upon the self; of descending backwards into the traditional subject-object dichotomy. Second, the self that exists within the world is a self that speaks, and, following the thought of Lacan, the subject that speaks (the je) is a spectacle that pushes itself further into the world in the form of signifiers, meaning and discourse.[4] In other words, when the self speaks, it posits itself closer to the Other that it exists beside, pressing itself upon the world as a meaning. Speech is the 'accomplishment' of the speaker's thoughts.[5] Third, speech is an expression of desire and narcissism, governed by a logic of desire and narcissism, which opens the subject as a loss of what it had been, replacing itself in the world with its speech, and pushing itself further into the world in an expression of power.[6]

WHEN THE TECHNOLOGICAL DEVICE BECOMES A HABITUAL OBJECT, IT CEASES ITS FUNCTION AS AN OBJECT OUTSIDE OF THE BODY AND BECOMES A PART OF THE BODY ITSELF.

What does it mean, then, for the self to adopt an appendage as part of itself? The adoption of a new

appendage to the self is to enhance the vehicle of experience that is the body, i.e., to add to the perceptual self, thereby altering the self's interaction within the world. By altering the extensions of the body via technology, one affects the very process of sense experience itself.[7] Merleau-Ponty expounds upon this point through his example of the blind man's use of a stick:

> The blind man's stick has ceased to be an object for him, and is no longer perceived for itself; its point has become an area of sensitivity, extending the scope and active radius of touch, and providing a parallel to sight...To get used to a hat, a car or a stick is to be transplanted into them, or conversely, to incorporate them into the bulk of our own body. Habit expresses our power of dilating our being in the world, or changing our existence by appropriating fresh instruments.[8]

This quoted passage not only reveals the phenomena of the body's extensions, but the importance of *habit* in acquiring these extensions as manipulations of the self. The effectiveness of the t-meme in becoming an acquired appendage is its habitual use. When the technological device becomes a habitual object, it ceases its function as an object outside of the body and becomes a part of the body itself. In other words, it becomes an aspect of the self, thereby altering the self from what it previously was. "We say that the body has understood and habit has been cultivated when it has absorbed a new meaning, and assimilated a fresh core of significance."[9]

With the acquisition of a new perceptual appendage, the self alters the *field* in which it exists. Not only does the physical existence of the appendage push itself out into the space otherwise unfilled, but new perceptual potentialities, actualities, and needs arise within the field that did not exist before. Suddenly data that were formerly unavailable become necessary, and this causes the subject to become dependent upon such data once it becomes both existent and habitually accessible. As John Dewey notes, the acquisition of new habits often 'cuts across some old habits,' thereby causing 'instability, novelty, emergence of unexpected and unpredictable combinations.'[10]

These instabilities and unpredictable combinations are most recognizable within the social sphere itself. Whereas the old habits of sociability were once standard and primary, the self finds itself suspended between the significance of both old habits and the new habits acquired due to the alteration of perceptual field. For example, I recently witnessed two young people out on a date. Half of the date was spent practicing the 'old habits' of dating: talking with one another, eating, drinking, so on and so forth. The other half consisted of one of the individuals focusing upon another field of perception, the field opened up by the new appendage, i.e., a cellular phone. What had occurred was the clashing of old habits with new, ultimately ending in a compromise between perceptual fields. The old habits dealt strictly with the 'here and now', whereas the new habits forced intentionality towards the 'there and now'. Within this situation alone, one could see the evolved cellph envelop the old self. The cellph differs from its former self not only in its acquisition of a new appendage and field of existence, but also in the split nature that is forced upon it by this acquisition.[11]

The subject that is the cellph is split into two forms of speaking subject in its role as self: a *private* subject participating in dialogue through the medium of its appendage and a *public* spectacle that is seen participating in a dialogue to which others outside of the appendage are forbidden access. Regarding desire, the former is an expression of the cellph's desire to be desired by a specific other. Not only is the narcissism of speaking involved in the dialogue, which the cellph is having with an-other ("Listen, specifically, to me."), but this desire for desire as well ("Desire to listen to me.").[12] In the latter, the cellph expresses this same desire for desire ("Desire to listen to me."), but not the same narcissism. Rather, there is an expression of 'not being allowed' to listen to the dialogue, which the others hear as a monologue, while there is also the expression of 'being allowed' to watch the cellph speaking to an-other

BOTH OLD HABITS AND THE SHAPE OF THE 'OLD WORLD' ARE BEING OVERTHROWN DUE TO THIS EVOLUTION.

("Watch, specifically, me."). In other words, the cellph in the public sphere becomes both a forbidden (or restricted) aural spectacle and temptation while enhancing its place as an (overly) accessible visual spectacle.

The cellph is split regarding its knowledge as well. The appendage becomes necessary for storing information that has to do with both the field of perception which it causes to emerge and fields of perception outside of itself. Phone numbers, bank account information, e-mail, documents, and even dates[13] are stored within so that the cellph need not store them within the brain. The cellular phone becomes an extension of the brain, i.e., an extension of the memory system itself. In this regard the cellular phone as technological appendage has not only manipulated perception and its field, but also the very *episteme* of the subject. With evolution comes an alteration of knowledge. The cellph is a different *knower* than the self.

In order to compensate for this knowledge stored within an appendage outside of the brain, the cellph becomes dependent not only upon the cellular phone, but also upon ways of keeping it attached to its-cellph. Purses, backpacks, and winter coats are now constructed with pockets for carrying the new appendage; even blazers for business are being tailored to ensure constant contact with the new perceptual field.[14] Vehicles even accommodate the need for being 'there and now' while traveling in the 'here and now' to another 'there'. With the demise of the self, the world undergoes a necessary alteration to accommodate the cellph. Both old habits and the shape of the 'old world' are being overthrown due to this evolution.

Before closing, one more example of the oddity of the new cellph must be given. Sitting in a café one afternoon, I witnessed a middle-aged couple come in, order drinks, and sit down. The entirety of their stay was spent with each one talking on cellular phones. As they both got up to leave, each looked at the other, and then they embraced and kissed. After a rather overt display of physical affection, they walked from the café hand in hand. Soon after this incident, I began wondering if they were talking to one another through this new technological appendage; if each had acquired the new habits of the cellph to such a strong degree that there was no other possibility for verbal communication. Perhaps we are witnessing both the antiquation and the extinction of certain perceptual fields in favor of new fields opened up by our acquisition of technological appendages. Perhaps the mouth is no longer directly connected to the ear, now needing a cellular filter in order to be heard or acknowledged.

---

1 T-memes include the wheel, fire, automobiles, air conditioning, and computers, as well as others.

2 "Examples of memes are tunes, ideas, catchphrases, clothes fashions, ways of making pots or of building arches." Dawkins, R. *The Selfish Gene*. (Oxford: Oxford University Press), 1976. 206.

3 Merleau-Ponty, M. *Philosophy of Perception*. Trans. Smith, C. (London: Routledge & Kegan Paul), 1962. 96.

4 Ragland-Sullivan, *Lacan and the Philosophy of Psychoanalysis*. (Champaign : University of Illinois Press), 1987. 212.

5 Merleau-Ponty, 178.

6 Ragland-Sullivan, 182.

7 Merleau-Ponty, 52.

8 Ibid, 143.

9 Ibid, 146.

10 Dewey, J. *Experience and Nature*. (Open Court: La Salle, IL), 1958. 229-30.

11 Some of the points in this passage could also be made for the use of internet technologies, especially in regards to real-time 'chatting.' However, due to the public spectacle of cellular phone use, the split of the cellph is more apparent than the split that occurs with the acquisition of an internet 'chatself.'

12 "Desire always becomes manifest at the joint of speech, where it makes its appearance, its sudden emergence, its surge forwards. Desire emerges just as it becomes embodied in speech, it emerges with symbolism." Lacan, J. *The Seminar of Jacques Lacan: Book II, The Ego in Freud's Theory and in the Technique of Psychoanalysis, 1954-55*. Ed. Miller, J.-A. Trans. Tomaselli, S. (New York: W.W. Norton & Co.), 1991. 234.

13 I know of one individual who had to store the date of his significant other's birthday in his phone so that he could remember it.

14 I thank Kyle West for pointing this new phenomenon out to me.

Purchase *your* subscription or increasingly rare back Issues of BRIDGE

Bridge 1

Kurt Vonnegut (interview), Rennie Sparks, John Domini, Cheryl Trykv, Neil Pollack, Paul Maliszewski, Colette Inez (interview), Reginald Gibbons, Maxine Chernoff, Susie Timmons, Thax Douglas, Monica Kendrick & others.

Bridge 2

Aimee Bender, Michael Martone, Mary Jo Bang, Paul Hoover, Greg Purcell, Paula Kamen, Paul Maliszewski, Chris Johansen, Archer Prewitt, Katy Fischer, Jim Hanas, Todd Dills & others.

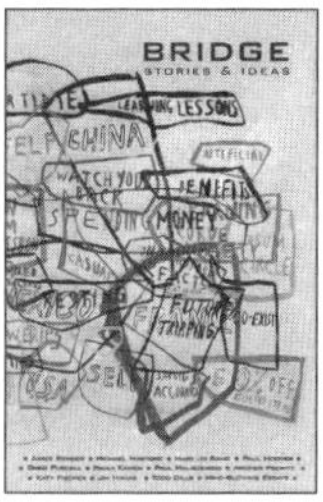

Bridge 3

Frances Sherwood, Wislawa Szymborska, Tim W. Brown, Wayne C. Booth, John Keene, Rebecca Wolff, Cris Mazza, Mike Newirth, Gary Pike, Art Shay, Mark Wallace, Law Office & others + CD including: John Barth, The Goblins, Jim Munroe, Cheryl Trykv, Negativland, Ashtray Boy, Jon Langford, Colette Inez, Janice Eidus, L.D. Beghtol's Moth Wranglers, Lawrence Krauser & others.

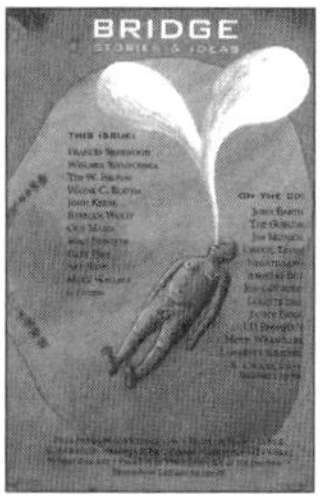

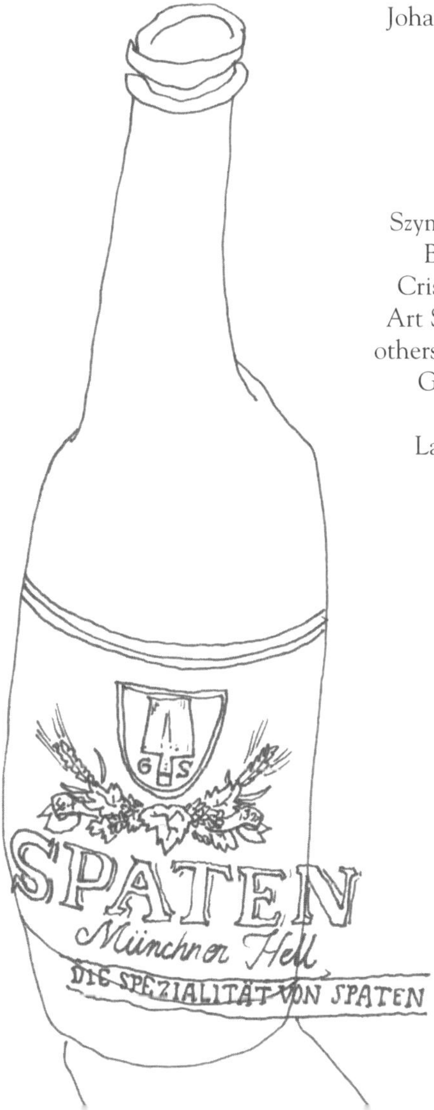

Subscriptions

Individuals: $17.00; foreign, add $3.50

Institutions: $26.00; foreign, add $3.50

Bridge 1—$10

Bridge 2—$10

Bridge 3—$15

To order by credit card, please visit www.bridgemagazine.org

(Please add $2 to all orders of back issues for S&H)

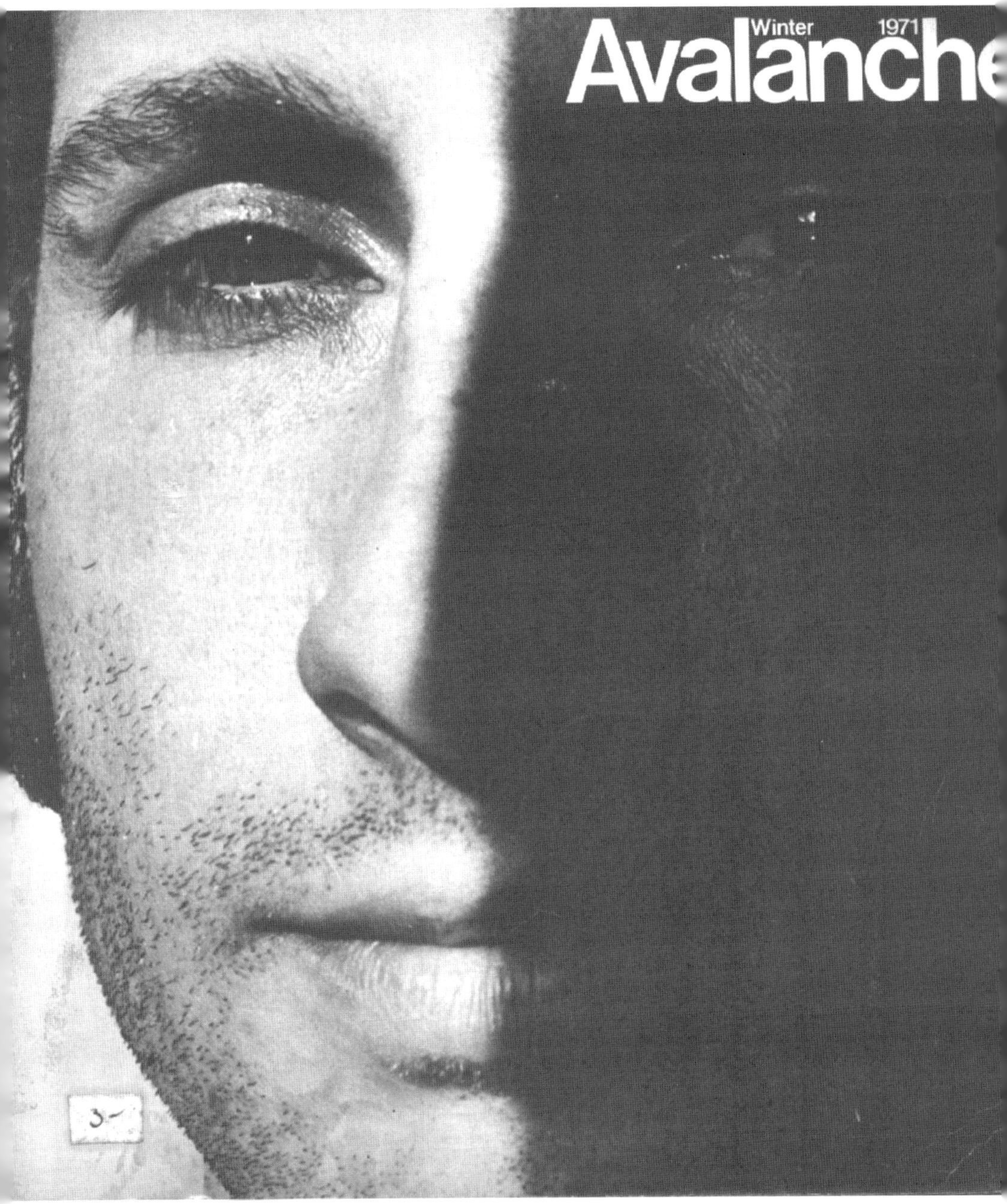

Bruce Nauman cover photo by Gianfranco Gorgoni

IDEAL AVALANCHE

Michelle Grabner and Brad Killam

Having taken the opportunity to clean out the home office recently, we dusted off and rediscovered a handful of early 1970's issues of *Avalanche*. Published by writer and video pioneer Willoughby Sharpe, *Avalanche* stands among early issues of *Artforum* and *Arts Magazine* as an indispensable publication documenting an era of artistic activity generally regarded as minimal and conceptual. Featuring interviews, essays and advertisements that embraced the dynamic production of such contemporary luminaries as Chris Burden, Lawrence Wiener, Jackie Winsor, William Wegman, Gilbert and George, Alice Aycock, Bruce Naumen, Vito Acconci, Hanna Darbovan, Gordon Matta Clark, Robert Smithson and Richard Serra among others, *Avalanche*, like the companion forementioned publications, championed the radical positions of the day and laid the groundwork for a model of critical dialogue in print. The magazine's circulation life now long forgotten, it remains an inspiring, authoritative, if hard to find, document of authentic colloquy between artists.

Lawrence Wiener at Amsterdam: an interview excerpt by Willoughby Sharpe with Lawrence Weiner, May 15, 1971, Amsterdam (*Avalanche*, Winter 1972, pp. 68, 69):

WS: You assume I have the same precepts about art as you do.

LW: They are the general cultural precepts of western art. I can only deal in western art because I'm a westerner.

WS: Then what are the general cultural precepts that you assume other people share?

LW: The basis of cultural history until now.

WS: Well, that's very vague.

LW:No, it's not, it's very specific, meaning what has shaped your culture and mine.

WS: There are very few people that accept a certain sentence as art.

LW: "Very few people" doesn't mean anything.

WS: You're assuming a lot. You assume I agree with . . .

LW: I haven't said that I assume that you agree or disagree. When you deal with a piece of mine, you come across a sentence. It is just verbal.

WS: It could be.

What then is missing in today's periodicals compared to *Avalanche*? The most obvious is the manner which artworks and artists' overall projects are discussed. It hasn't gone unnoticed that a good portion of critical discussion regarding art production in today's art glossies is assigned to the reviews department. There, at least, one has a chance to engage a critical position. All too often, however, many periodicals resort to a basic description and cheerleading format for their five hundred word reviews. This leaves little room for robust debate or full on arguments. *Avalanche*, by contrast was structured without a reviews section. Its format was comprised of mostly interviews, discussions among artists and artists' projects. This allowed the editors and artists the opportunity for disagreements and candid debate. Sometimes transcripts from early video work or photo documentation of performances or site work would be given generous coverage. The artists' published projects for the magazine were sometime hard to distinguished from the full page black and white ads that were extentions of artistic ideas rather then gallery-promotion.

Excepts from <u>Vito Acconci, September 27, 1971</u> a single page project (*Avalanche* Fall 1971 page 78):

This page is like a training ground: writing here is like preparing myself.

Writing here is like nodding my head—a token of my readiness to the person who will call me into activity. This is my only means of contacting her. She can't be someone I already know, or someone I meet casually, in the future: I should know her only in terms of this situation: this page should cause our relationship.

The standards once set by dialogues and ideological positions in art magazines has all but given way to features like *Artforum's* "Best of 2001." And, since those top ten lists say almost nothing in regards to a philosophical position regarding any of the artists, then readers should assume that the editors are making shopping lists for curators and collectors. These 20 pages of top ten lists create a competitive structure not a discursive one.

<u>Bruce Naumen:</u> an interview excerpt by Willoughby Sharpe with Bruce Nauman on May 7, 1970 (*Avalanche*, Winter 1971, pp. 30, 31):

WS: Would you like to do something for network TV?

BN: I'd like CBS to give me an hour on my terms. I'd like to do color work which I haven't done yet because of the expense involved. Some people in Europe have been able to use it. I forget who. A Dutch artists did something called the Television as a Fireplace. Apparently a fire was broadcast on the screen for fifteen minutes or so. All you saw was fire.

WS: Do you feel that you could subvert television, change it?

BN: I'm not really interested in actively spending my time trying to get those people to let me use their time. If time was offered to me I would use it, and I would want to do things my way. But to take the time to do whatever one has to do . . .

WS: So there really isn't a strong desire to change the existing level of communication?

BN: No.

WS: Then we come back to where we ended the last time: who is art for?

BN: To keep me busy.

The state of artistic practice as represented in current art glossies highlights a tectonic shift in the perception of artistic practice. Younger generations, awkwardly influenced by the lack of dialogue in art magazines, perceive their "job" as being one of making a career as opposed to being an artist.

A description of two actions by Chris Burden (*Avalanche* Summer/Fall 1973 pp.54, 56):

Five Day Locker Piece, April 26-30, 1971, Irvine California, Photo: Diana Zlotnik.

I was locked in locker No. 5 for five consecutive days and did not leave the locker during this time. The locker measurements were 2 ft. high, 2 ft. wide, 3 ft. deep. I stopped eating several days prior to entry, thereby eliminating the problem of solid waste. The locker directly above me contained five gallons of bottled water; the locker below me contained an empty 5 gallon bottle. The photograph shows all threee lockers; number 5 is in the middle.

I Became A Secret Hippie, October 3, 1971, MOCA, San Francisco. Photograph Barbara Burden.

The Piece began when I took off all my clothes —jeans and t-shirt—and lay on the floor on my back. A friend hammered a star shaped stud into my sternum. I then sat in chair and had all my hair cut off. Finally, I dressed in the clothes shown in the photograph.

Historian and critic, Lane Relyea delivered a paper titled "It's the End Of Art Criticism As We Know It (And The Art World Feels Fine)," to an audience at the Museum of Fine Arts Houston in October of 2001. Here he described art's critical and social polemics:

It's now popular to imagine today's artworld as made up of scenes (an L.A. scene, a London scene, a Tokyo scene, etc.); that is, we'd like to imagine our practices as unified by social rather than institutional or discursive forces. We don't read postmodern theory anymore, and we don't critique institutions; what we do is hang out.

The breath of contemporary art and the slippage of studio practice into all forms of visual cultural have made dynamic and contentious dialogue among artists less important than lightweight conversations with musicians, interior designers, fashion houses and the like. The result of this visual interfacing has produced a plethora of visual product magazines that are influencing the look and content of today's art periodicals. The new magazines look to promote as Relyea articulates, "hanging out," not ideologically fighting-it-out.

Sol Lewitt Page Drawings (*Avalanche*, Spring 1972 p. 18):

On this page using a pencil or a pen, draw lines from each vowel in this paragraph to each corner of this page.

Drinking Sculpture by Gilbert and George, an excerpt from a photographic project (*Avalanche*, Summer/Fall 1973, pp. 26-33):

Had two dizzy spells at lunch today. Asked two identical waiters to bring us a couple of doubles for the second time. Felt twice as good.

The opportunity to advance contemporary dialogue, then, lies in models like the pages of the modestly formatted, black and white *Avalanche*. That is to say that we need to reflect upon a generation of artists emerging in the late 1960's and early 1970's who launched their debates and positions, theories and actions publicly in print. What happened to the struggle of trying to finish-off painting in hopes to then assist in its resurrection? Does the desire to work against and beyond Brancusi, Giaccometti, Caro and Serra exist? Monumental questions have always consumed artists, in practice and print. In some rational but slow moving moment we seem to be struggling to find a forward driving discussion. Given ample time circumstances are bound to change. And the next time we clean out the home office we'll surely dust off another important contribution.

Lawrence Weiner cover photo by Doug Connor.

The Review of Contemporary Fiction

GILBERT SORRENTINO

NUMBER

Spring 1981

BRIDGE CRITICAL PORTFOLIO: GILBERT SORRENTINO AND THE REVIEW OF CONTEMPORARY FICTION

"Something Has Sure As Hell Happened": Gilbert Sorrentino, *The Review of Contemporary Fiction*, and Provocative Fiction

David Andrews

In Hal Hartley's film *Henry Fool* (1998), Simon Grimm, an uneducated garbage-man, writes a poem whose power is clarified by the responses it generates. One literary magazine is so moved by the poem that it departs from its standard rejection-letter protocol: "Every week we are forced to return writing which we cannot for one reason or another publish and include a brief but polite refusal. But this tract you sent us demands a response as violent as the effect your words have had upon us. Drop dead! Keep your day job!" Thereafter, a school board labels the poem "scatological," a parents' association dubs it "pornography," and a politician delivers a hysterical, televised denunciation. Even approving readers react violently: for instance, a group of students torch a school, and Simon's mother commits suicide. Perhaps the most comic responses are physiological. A mute suddenly bursts into song. Simon's sister gets her period early. As the narrator of Kurt Vonnegut's *Bluebeard* (1987) says of an equally controversial artwork, Simon's poem is "terribly important the same way a head-on collision is important . . . There's undeniable impact. Something has sure as hell happened" (281).

A similar dynamic, it seems, has long informed responses to Gilbert Sorrentino's output. Is it a cliché to point out that readers either love or hate his work, with few fence-sitters? Having just finished teaching his novel *Imaginative Qualities of Actual Things* (1971) to a class at the University of Illinois at Chicago, I know whereof I speak: though many students enjoyed the book's ferocious comedy,[1] an equal number were visibly flustered by its dark, sardonic, always explicit obsession with the sexual (and typically adulterous) habits of the New York artworld of the 1950s and 60s. But the content wasn't the only thing that upset my students. A few seemed *mad* that the novel comprised a bricolage of lists and letters and marginalia, with the narrative mostly relayed via sketches-within-sketches. "Why doesn't he just tell the damn story?" Such palpable seething reminded me of the day almost ten years ago that I first encountered Sorrentino in a doctoral seminar at SUNY Stony Brook. That week the focus was *Aberration of Starlight* (1980). I was in the minority, defending (not loudly enough, as I recall) the book's modernist architecture against a group of peers who, naturally, had liberal

[1] On the positive side, one of my students, Jonathan Joyce, who happens to be the great-nephew of a certain James Joyce, paid me the ultimate compliment of noting that reading *Imaginative Qualities* and *Lolita*—the latter a book that the narrator of *Imaginative Qualities* mocks most mercilessly—had given him a newfound appreciation for his great-uncle's books. High praise, indeed!

views on everything but aesthetics. They, too, wanted "storytelling," whatever that means, and were angered by Sorrentino's decision to repeat the same rudimentary story not just by relating it from four different viewpoints but by using ten stylistically distinct documents within each viewpoint. Nor did they care for his indecorous descent into "pornography" in a few sections, especially since *Aberration*'s sexual motifs did not indirectly express a familiar form of humanism. "It's just too much." In this context, the distinction suggested by "undergraduate" and "graduate" seems particularly arbitrary.

Perhaps I overstress the negative. After all, my own reaction, though positive, was no less extreme. Reading *Aberration* that day—in tandem with two other Sorrentino pieces, his essay "The Act of Creation And Its Artifact" and his interview with John O'Brien, i.e., the first piece in the first issue of *The Review of Contemporary Fiction*—encouraged me to read *Imaginative Qualities* on my own—and I was hooked. Afterward, I devoured all of Sorrentino's books. His work became a focus of my research and remains an insistent fascination. This story is not unique. I introduced a friend to Imaginative Qualities a year ago; not long after, he applied to a doctoral program where he will soon begin his study of contemporary American literature. Similarly, "Avant Guards," a *Reader* piece of 2 November 2001, tells of another man who, on reading *Imaginative Qualities*, transformed his life, eventually becoming a senior editor at the Dalkey Archive Press, the publishing affiliate of *The Review* (10).

Which brings me to the point of this special portfolio of essays, all of which pay homage to Sorrentino and the inaugural issue of *The Review*—a journal that, just over twenty years ago, first paid homage to Sorrentino. Though most of these critics praised his work, it wasn't hollow encomium, for *The Review* is unique in that it combines a scholarly approach with a more partisan mission to promote innovative fiction, whether by figures of established importance like Jack Kerouac or by chronically neglected figures like Coleman Dowell or David Markson. Considering that, as artist and critic, Sorrentino is both famously precise and famously partisan, *The Review*'s approach seems apt. Indeed, John O'Brien's establishment of *The Review* in 1981 and the Dalkey Archive Press in 1984 may constitute the most telling—and tremendous—response to Sorrentino and his work. Just as *The Review* lavished its initial energy on Sorrentino, so did Dalkey, which on its formation quickly reprinted *Splendide-Hôtel* (1973), his lyrical evocation of the corruption of contemporary art and culture. Since then, Dalkey has steadfastly kept his books in print, and evidence of his influence continues to register in such recent O'Brien projects as *Context*, a literary newspaper, and the umbrella operation known as the Center For Book Culture. Though Hartley's character ends up influencing the Nobel committee, Sorrentino's impact may be of a type that has greater significance, for he has quite plainly influenced a journal and a publishing concern that have in turn quietly reshaped the landscape for innovative fiction both in America and abroad.

Ironically, the quality that makes Sorrentino so uniquely powerful may be the one that relegates him to virtual anonymity among less accomplished peers. When he admires an author like Edward Dahlberg, Sorrentino occasionally compliments that author by observing that "he is not for sale"—a blandishment clearly true of himself. It is not that Sorrentino doesn't want his books to sell. On the contrary, throughout his criticism, he rages against publishers unwilling to promote idiosyncratic works and readers unwilling to buy them. Instead, unlike the poet Leo Kaufman in *Imaginative Qualities*, Sorrentino is unwilling to "surrender," to sell out, to compromise his art in the smallest particulars. Were I a psychologist rather than a critic (a distinction that critics make, it seems, all too seldom), I might speculate that he has experienced anxiety on this point, for his fictions do not simply suggest integrity, they often scream it. Thus the tendency of Sorrentino's narrators, whether in early novels like *Imaginative Qualities* or recent ones like *Under The Shadow* (1991), *Gold Fools* (2001), and *Little Casino* (2002),[2] to attack publishers and readers who demand compromise, and artists who, in acceding to such demands, create a genial, homogeneous art, a smiling art, an art of common denominators. It is as if Sorrentino wants his reader to be absolutely aware that though he intends to share his art with others, his artifacts, like Leo's best poems, are nevertheless "for himself" (151). Such a stance almost guarantees a strong reaction—though, while some readers will admire its unassailable integrity, others will call it arrogant, elitist.

Of course, it is not only the opinionated, proscriptive, and occasionally bristling posture of Sorrentino's narrators that express his integrity and that elicit such powerful reactions. As suggested, the innovative structures of his works also command response—and in this relation, it should be noted that *Imaginative Qualities* and *Aberration* are among his least difficult books. Sorrentino's best known novel, *Mulligan Stew* (1979), is a ludic collage of metafictive documents that seem in open competition with each other—yet none is ever validated or oriented by a controlling narrator. The novels published after *Aberration* are more difficult to describe—though many, especially those comprising the trilogy *Pack of Lies* (1997), involve complex literary structures that, like those of *Mulligan Stew*, are designed to destabilize notions of authenticity, of truth and fact, hence obfuscating the reader's pursuit of a reliable narrative information. In Sorrentino's short stories, which are mainly narrated in the first-person, a similar process is performed through a

[2] *Little Casino* will be released by Coffee House this May. It is a wonderful, immensely readable novel that, in its obssession with the past, is by turns ironic, self-reflexive, comic, poignant, cranky, and dark. It is comprised of narrative fragments whose subject matter resembles that of *Steelwork* (1970) and *Aberration of Starlight*; yet these fragments "hang together" in a way more reminiscent of *The Orangery* (1978), Sorrentino's finest book of poetry, or of *Under The Shadow*, a dreamy fiction in which contrapuntal motifs and narrative "bits" never quite coalesce into a "story" but instead wax and wane like a fugue.

continual investigation and complication of the notion of the stable self, of the "I" who speaks. Or consider three recent Sorrentino novels, all of which "translate" prior literary models. Thus *Under The Shadow* is an adaptation of H.A. Zo's illustrations in Raymond Roussel's *Nouvelles Impressions d'Afrique* (1932); *Red The Fiend* (1995) an adaptation of Jules Renard's *Poil de Carotte* (1893); and *Gold Fools* an adaptation of a boys' adventure book, Willard Baker's *The Boy Ranchers in the Desert* (1924). Put that in your pipe and smoke it, one might imagine the author saying.

But I don't think he is really saying that (which, I should confess, I remind myself whenever I read those two or three novels that, in their dogged opacity, can frustrate and fluster even me). If Sorrentino sometimes screams, he never postures. That is, he *really* isn't for sale. This doesn't entail his antipathy, his arrogance, etc. It simply means that he is an artist, and, more specifically, a comic artist, who sincerely enjoys writing not for what the product of that process will or will not bring him but for the experience itself. When he sees a new technique or problem that will manifest the kind of experience—and the kind of comic art—that he most enjoys, he simply explores it, heedless of the marketplace. (This attitude would make him more like a painter than a novelist except that painters do not, it seems, of necessity choose between innovation and marketability.) This view may be difficult to accept. Who the hell would want to parody a boys' adventure novel? Who would enjoy writing fifty-nine intersecting vignettes about fifty-nine banal drawings by Zo, a "hack draughtsman"? Still, to insist Sorrentino enjoy only the type of writing that one enjoys oneself seems to me guilty of the same self-indulgence that radical novelists are so automatically accused of. Plus, anyone who reads *Gold Fools* and *Under The Shadow* will realize that Sorrentino really *has* enjoyed the creative acts that yielded these fictions. Their nonstop hilarity confirms as much.

Beyond this fundamental fact, a more sophisticated set of attitudes has played a role in determining the complexity of Sorrentino's later fiction. He is a modernist, his early models having been Ezra Pound and William Carlos Williams. Moreover, he was part of the last flowering of modernism in America, having reached his artistic maturity in a 1950s Greenwich Village milieu where Abstract Expressionist painters, abstract-jazz musicians, and poets of the Black Mountain, New York, and San Francisco schools shared ideas. Like them, he insists on continual invention so that art will, as John Dewey puts it in *Art As Experience*, "do away with the scales that keep the eye

from seeing," so that it will "tear away the veils due to wont and custom" (325). This, at least, is easy to absorb. Sorrentino is a self-conscious modernist. Modernists innovate; that is what they do. Still, this tautology goes only so far in explaining the truly radical nature of his invention over the past decades. More helpful is framing him not simply as a modernist in the "make it new" mold but a modernist *aesthete* in that mold.

Sorrentino's aestheticism registers most vehemently via his gathering insistence on the "uselessness" of art, a notion that is a staple of his remarkable criticism.[3] Art is not a tool—which means it is not a signifier pointing to some idea beyond itself. Rather, art is a thing, a self-enclosed reality. Such a credo presents any artist with a formidable artistic problem; given the original signifying function of his medium, words, it presents a writer with a more formidable problem; and given that Sorrentino is by nature an opinionated, rhetorical writer, it presents *him* with perhaps the most formidable problem of all. What I am suggesting, then, is that the burgeoning strangeness of Sorrentino's poetry and fiction, beyond a straightforward expression of the joy he finds in writing for its own sake, is also a deliberate attempt to bring art into line with ideology. The strength of his ideas, of his natural voice, can only be broken up, scrambled, and transformed into a useless, anti-referential art by inventions of equal strength and complexity.

This idea is clarified by three novels from the 1970s, *Imaginative Qualities*, *Splendide-Hôtel*, and *Mulligan Stew*. In the first, Sorrentino gives his narrator his own opinions, reasoning that narrators are artificial constructs and thus can never be confused with their authors. Still, the caustic satire of *Imaginative Qualities* on first glance comes across as didactic, even if (as Sorrentino and Toby Olson assure us) this is the wrong way to read the novel. After all, aren't the narrator's arguments in favor of uselessness *useful?* In its "arty" alphabetical structure, *Splendide-Hôtel* reveals Sorrentino wrestling with this problem. Though the narrator is stable and unitary—and his opinions still discernibly his author's—the book's structural artifice results in a cooler, more Olympian tone. *Mulligan Stew* is a breakthrough in that it dispenses with the question of didacticism altogether. Though Sorrentino admits that *Mulligan Stew* contains more autobiographical material than any of his works, this has gone unnoticed, perhaps because the novel's proliferating documents remain uncontrolled by a central voice, making it impossible to authorize or contextualize their constituent assertions. Ergo, in moving from *Imaginative Qualities* to *Mulligan Stew*, Sorrentino marshals increasingly exotic (and postmodernist) structures in his quest for forms that allow him to use his own ideas and

---

[3] An expanded *Something Said: Essays by Gilbert Sorrentino* was released by the Dalkey Archive in 2001. For a survey of this edition, see the review that appears in this issue of *Bridge*.

experiences without vitiating his aestheticist (and modernist) ideal of the autonomous artwork.

I could say more in this direction—I could, for instance, argue that *Pack of Lies* puts epistemological deconstruction in the service of artistic idealism, an unusual tactic for a modernist yet a predictable one given Sorrentino's aestheticist stance—but perhaps I've said enough. The last thing I want is to make him seem dull by blanketing him in fustian. Believe it: he is never dull. Even as his poems and novels evolve according to a deepening aestheticism, becoming more overtly artificial in the process, they are always animated by a blistering comedy and a vision of American experience whose prodigious bleakness results from a total rejection of humanism and its formulaic consolations. Here the late Richard Elman, my former teacher and a contributor to the first issue of *The Review*, is instructive in arguing that Sorrentino's aestheticism

> should be contemplated for what it is: the means by which an artist of great seriousness, and talent, and ability, has shaped the pain of experience to animate language and show the limitations by which we live, and the dramatic breaks, and small startling changes, and terrible betrayals. (156)

My initial point was that Sorrentino's integrity, as manifested by his unyielding opinions, his innovation, and his growing insistence on "uselessness," is at once the source of his power and, regrettably, the guarantor of his obscurity. Naturally, I hope I am wrong about that last part, for only if readers encounter his work will they get to shout their yea or nay as emphatically as he has. To twist one of Richard Rorty's phrasings, the goal of such persistent shouting is to force reality to admit, once and for all, that it has been *dented*—thus, as if by miracle, transforming the obscure into the classic.

The essays that follow all testify to the evocative, and often provocative, power of Sorrentino's imagination. They also acknowledge the contributions of *The Review* (not to mention the Dalkey Archive) to the dialogue surrounding his oeuvre and to the dialogue currently surrounding innovative contemporary fiction more generally. Two of the essayists, Toby Olson and Nicholas Mosley, are distinguished literary innovators in their own right. More to the point, both men contributed to the inaugural issue of *The Review* and have graciously agreed to revisit that experience in the pages of *Bridge*. By contrast, Jerome Klinkowitz and Robert McLaughlin are both accomplished scholars familiar with *The Review* and with Sorrentino: Klinkowitz through academic and personal relations with O'Brien and Sorrentino, McLaughlin through his ongoing editorship of *The Review*. While I do not agree with everything said in the following pages—for instance, *contra* Klinkowitz, I have seen *actual footage* of Sorrentino dissolving in laughter—I do agree with the energy with which everything said gets said. It is our hope at *Bridge* that this energy encourages more readers to read and respond in kind.

Sorrentino Bookends: *The Review of Contemporary Fiction*, the Academy, and Literary Culture

Robert L. McLaughlin

In Spring 1981, the first issue of *The Review of Contemporary Fiction*, focusing on the fiction of Gilbert Sorrentino, was published by John O'Brien, acting pretty much as a free agent. In September 2001, the third issue of the twenty-first volume of *The Review*, containing, among other things, an overview essay on Gilbert Sorrentino, by David Andrews, was published, and, while John O'Brien is still editor and publisher, much else has changed. *The Review* is now only one of the publishing efforts of the Dalkey Archive Press, a nonprofit publisher dedicated to publishing and—very important—keeping in print formally and stylistically innovative fiction. Other connected activities, incorporated under an umbrella organization, the Center for Book Culture, include *Context*, a tabloid publication focusing on the tradition of aesthetic innovation, and an active web site, which publishes interviews with authors and a series of on-line casebooks on novels like William Gass's *The Tunnel*, Carole Maso's *AVA*, and Flann O'Brien's *At Swim-Two-Birds*. Things can change a lot in twenty years.

This set of Sorrentino bookends, bracketing twenty years of *The Review*, offers an opportunity to think a bit about what else has changed—about the journal, about the study of contemporary fiction, about the state of innovative literature in a mass-market culture—during this time. I've been Senior Editor of *The Review*, responsible for the bulk of each issue's content, since 1993. In looking back at that first issue, which I hadn't seen in some time and which is kind of hard to get a hold of (issue #1 is scarce even in the Dalkey Archive offices—there's one copy, under lock and key, armed guard, very intimidating), I was surprised at how familiar it was. Upon further reflection, I realized I really shouldn't have been, as it was, after all, the model for all the issues of *The Review*—with the exception of the occasional fiction issue or special-themed issue—until 2000. There was an interview with Sorrentino, a critical piece by him (the first published appearance of his "The Act of Creation and Its Artifact"), a selection from a work-in-progress (*Blue Pastoral*). There too were an autobiographical reminiscence by a fellow author, Hubert Selby, and several general appreciations by other men of letters—Coleman Dowell, Nicholas Mosley, Richard Elman, Robert Creeley. Mostly, there were short essays by literary critics offering interpretive angles with which to approach specific Sorrentino works, with a heavy emphasis on *Mulligan Stew*.

What seemed most different about the issue were the generally cranky book reviews, including a pan of Puig's *Kiss of the Spiderwoman*. Nowadays, we try to use our book-review space to draw attention to worthy, out-of-the-commercial-mainstream books that might not otherwise be found by our readers, our reasoning being: Why print a review telling readers that they shouldn't read a book they probably wouldn't hear about anyway? Also interesting were the number of reviews that complained about books being out-of-print and calling on publishers to recognize their duties to print important, if less popular, fiction. I could be wrong, but I'm guessing that many of these reviews were written by a pseudonymous John O'Brien. It's interesting to see this early the concerns that would be the seeds for the Dalkey Archive.

But in general one can see in the Sorrentino issue the virtues of and the problems with the format for which it served as model. On the virtue side of the equation, it provided—in the interview, the critical article, the work-in-progress—a healthy sampling of the author's voice. Since the assumption here is that many of the readers won't have been familiar with the author, what better way to introduce him than through his own words? It also provides a number of takes on the author by other authors, rather than literary critics, which, since fiction writers tend to approach and respond to fiction differently from academics, offer different kinds of insights. It also provides a variety of compact readings of the author's major works by literary critics, readings valuable both for their contributions to the ongoing scholarly work about the author and for the interpretive models they offer the reader new to his work. On the problem side of the equation—perhaps less problems than challenges that could become problems as we put together the many post-Sorrentino issues—getting the interview, critical piece, and work-in-progress from the featured author wasn't always easy, especially when the author was a) dead, b) ill-tempered, c) uncooperative, d) all of the above. Getting authors to write on other authors can be hard (they're busy, understandably; they have nothing to say about author X; they've contributed to the last several issues), and the line between genuine appreciation (i.e., critical insight) and general appreciation (i.e., blah, blah, blah) is thinner than you'd think. Getting academics to write *compact*

readings of the featured author's work is hard both because academics tend not to think in terms of compact when they're writing and because the balance of the creation of new scholarship with writing for the nonspecialized novice is difficult to maintain—if you don't believe me, try it. There's also the coordination problem, getting the various contributors to cover the featured author's opus evenly—as I noted earlier, in issue #1 there are a lot of *Mulligan Stew* articles at the expense of some of Sorrentino's other novels.

This isn't to suggest that *The Review*'s editors, guest editors, and contributors didn't turn out a lot excellent author issues over the years, but it starts to explain why we moved to a new format a couple of years back. Along with the above editorial/administrative challenges, O'Brien and I began to wonder if the tried-and-true format was the best way to present some of the authors we wanted to treat, some of them authors (like Sorrentino) whom we had already done but who had turned out significant new work since their issues and some of them younger authors who hadn't turned out a lot of fiction yet but who deserve critical attention. The result of our musing was the move to a new format: each author is treated in a long essay that covers the intellectual biography and influences, the critical reception and scholarly conversations, and interpretive approaches to the major works. As before, our emphasis is on authors who have received less attention than they deserve and our imagined audience is intelligent but not necessarily academic specialists. The Fall 2001 issue is a nice example, I think, of the potential for this format. Two essays return to authors who had previously been subjects of old-style author issues: Sorrentino, by Andrews, and William Gaddis, by John Beer (there's also Andrews's interview with Sorrentino, not a regular feature of the new format, but we couldn't resist). A third essay (by, ahem, me) focuses on Mary Caponegro, a really interesting younger author who has received nowhere near the popular and critical attention she deserves. The final essay, by Joy Castro, covers the career of Margery Latimer, an almost-forgotten writer of the twenties and thirties. These essays go about their business in different ways, but they all succeed in making the case for their subjects' importance and in offering critical and interpretive approaches to their work.

Looking more broadly at the twenty-year span between the two treatments of Sorrentino in *The Review*, I see reflected in our issues some of the changes that have occurred in our profession. The early essays tend to be formal readings, focusing on the aesthetics of the featured author and/or the structural means by which he or she creates fiction. Farther into the Years of Theory, the essays often foreground discussions of aesthetic, interpretive, and epistemological assumptions, which, at their best, connect the featured author's work to broader networks of philosophical and cultural thought and, at their not-so-best, use the featured author as a pretext to gallop on a theoretical hobbyhorse. One can also call these the Years of Jargon and the Endnote, during which a well-read-intelligent-but-not-academic-specialist reader seemed impossible for many academics to imagine, and so readability really became an issue in the sense that it runs counter to *The Review*'s mission to imply that the fiction we advocate can be appreciated only by the small company of professorial specialists. Recently, I've seen with relief that more and more of the bright young people earning their Ph.D.s in contemporary literature have their theory under their belts without feeling the need to flaunt (or flog) it and take pride in setting sophisticated analyses and arguments in graceful, readable prose. A connected observation, though, is that the rise of cultural studies, while liberating in the sense that it throws open the door to a whole world of texts and discourses—not just literary texts—as legitimate objects of study, also means that a large number of scholars who might have brought their critical intelligences to bear on the Caponegros, the David Foster Wallaces, the Richard Powerses, and the William T. Vollmanns—the way a previous generation of scholars did on Pynchon, Barth, Vonnegut, and the gaggle of High Postmodernists—are instead pursuing other things. For some of these Bourdieu-invoking scholars, *aesthetics* is a dirty word and those of us still interested in literature as a special kind of discourse are objects of pity or contempt. This state of professional affairs is in some ways exciting and in some ways depressing (as when I see my own interests and work demeaned), but most relevant here, it confirms for me the need for *The Review*, its philosophy and its praxis.

But there is a still broader sense in which this continued need for *The Review*'s mission is less than inspiring. In issue #1's interview with Sorrentino, much is made of his small readership. In Fall 2001's interview, the difficulty of his getting his novels published is stressed. This makes me wonder (here I am getting depressed again) how much good we do if, after twenty years, Gilbert Sorrentino is still having trouble getting published, still inspiring only a modest readership, still generating only a trickle of literary criticism. Of course, one must think of this in the context of the larger literary culture, and, boy, that's where things have really changed in the last twenty years. When the first issue of *The Review* came out, we were just beginning the age of conglomeratization: then, we had many commercial publishers, middle-sized businesses, each with its own style, interests, and quirky tastes; today, those publishers are miniscule revenue sources of the A.O.L.-Time-Warner-Disney-Bertelsmann-type multinational corporations. In 1981, Waldenbooks and B. Dalton were just starting to strike it rich by modeling their mall stores after the CVS. Now not only do we have the

Borders and Barnes and Noble superstores, we have the Internet and the thousands upon thousands of books available to anyone with a computer and a credit card. You'd think this was good—more books, more means of getting them into people's hands—but never in the history of publishing has there been less motivation on the part of publishers (and their Gargantuan parents) and bookstores to promote innovative or experimental literature over commercially safe books. That they sometimes do is something of a miracle, and miracles don't happen every day. The commercial literary marketplace is almost completely about the selling—not the reading—of books. How many commercially published books do you read that aren't rife with typos? I honestly think no one at the conglomeratized publishers expects anyone to read their books.

The bright side to all this is that this hypercommercialization of the literary marketplace has inspired a reaction: the growth of a vigorous nonprofit literary publishing movement, of which the Dalkey Archive and *The Review* are a part. If the commercial publishing industry has abrogated its responsibility to literary culture, that responsibility hast been assumed by small publishers, who, thanks to governmental, institutional, and foundational support, are not answerable to the marketplace. The optimistic answer to the Sorrentino situation is that while he may still be having trouble getting published and his novels aren't coming out from Random House, he is nevertheless being published and most of his books are in print and available to readers, and there's at least one journal that studies and celebrates his fiction and the fiction of other innovative authors. In the cacophony of our commercialized literary culture, there are some small voices acclaiming, missionary-style, the possibilities of an oppositional, avant-garde aesthetic. *The Review of Contemporary Fiction* is one of them. Things can change a lot in twenty years, but we'll keep doing what we've been doing, thanks.

The Review of Contemporary Fiction

Nicholas Mosley

I first heard of plans for *The Review of Contemporary Fiction* in 1977 when John O'Brien wrote to me out of the blue to say he was thinking of doing a series of interviews with contemporary novelists, and he would like to include an interview with me. John was in Illinois, and I was in London, so my interview would have to be done by post: this was accomplished between 1978 and 1980. The first number of *The Review* came out in 1981 and was dedicated to Gilbert Sorrentino, of whose work I had not known until John put me in touch with it. I read *Imaginative Qualities of Actual Things* and *Mulligan Stew*; and I wrote a piece on Sorrentino for the first number of *The Review*.

I greatly admired *Mulligan Stew*, which was a hugely inventive and ebullient work that went beyond the bounds of traditional fiction in trying to present the experience of human consciousness not as simplified convention would have it, but in its bewildering complexity. I had been trying myself to do something of the kind—which was why, presumably, I found myself in the company of the other authors in *The Review*. But it seemed to me that I, an Englishman, although I had been dubbed "experimental," was still in a different tradition to that of most of the Americans of whom Gilbert Sorrentino was such a striking leader. Sorrentino's style was exuberant, effervescent, spilling over with jokes, parodies, lists, haphazard juxtapositions. I had been trying to pare my fiction down so that the complexities I was trying to deal with might become visible through a sort of transparency.

I praised *Mulligan Stew* for its wit and insight. I wrote—"Either you, the readers, see that almost all your conventional ways of seeing things, reading about things, writing about things, are parodies, or you yourself will evaporate into a sort of parody yourself." And I quoted Nietzsche—"Objection, evasion, happy distrust, pleasure in mockery, are signs of health: everything unconditional belongs to pathology."

But then—"The problem is, as always, how to make an artwork of all this: how to communicate in writing the realisation that writing has conventionally become a purveyor of lies, but that this realisation is truthful." And I said that while reading *Mulligan Stew* it was not always easy to hold on to this; and I found myself turning from time to time to the photograph of Sorrentino himself on the cover as he glared out belligerently on his bemused and bemusing world. I did this in order to reassure myself of the reality, the authenticity, at least of the author.

In the summer of 1982, John O'Brien's interview with me was published, and in this I said more about my own efforts to express something of these ideas. That is—If one holds onto being aware that many of our everyday ways of seeing things are illusions, then what survives this has the chance of not being an illusion. And so on. Such a style is in danger of becoming tricky and manipulative, just as ebullience can become turgid and overflowing. But if literature is to be more than fantasy-gratification stories, then it seemed to me some such efforts had to be made. John O'Brien and *The Review*, and later the Dalkey Archive Press, seemed miraculously willing to embrace such genuine efforts; and the Press became and has remained my loyal publisher over the years.

I did not always keep up with what *The Review* was doing—it was hard enough to hold on to one's own struggles to combine artistry with intelligibility. But throughout the years of modernism, postmodernism, deconstruction, and so on, *The Review* has provided a platform for experiment, for variation, for criticism and commendation; and these were years when so-called "serious" fiction was finding it harder and harder to get an airing. But *The Review* and the Press flourished: and it seemed there was something to be learned here about the content of experiment, as well as style.

In the heady days of modernism in which James Joyce was what would nowadays be called an icon, the emphasis was all on style. *Ulysses* depended on its brilliancy of style: Bloom did not ruminate on meanings: in fact, meaning-of-life was soon to become a Monty Python joke. This was perhaps a valid defense against threats of falsity, authoritarianism, moral imposition. But then what was being recognised seemed to be a danger inherent in language (Wittgenstein—"Philosophy is a battle against the bewitchment of our intelligence by means of language"). What human beings cared about, struggled with, remained much the same.

It seemed to me that if literature apart from fantasy-wish-fulfillment was to have a future with a reasonable readership, then experiment had to be with ideas as well as with style. I do not know what Gilbert Sorrentino has done since his battling days of *Mulligan Stew*: most of the writers I admired in those days seem to have ceased—J.D. Salinger; John Fowles—or are there typescripts piling up in cupboards? These authors might have lost heart because of the lonely vulnerability of dealing with complexities and enigmas.

In the 1980 Marion Boyars edition of *Mulligan Stew*, there is printed a selection of letters of rejection that the book had elicited from publishers. Most of them are saying—We can see that this book is amazing, perhaps a work of genius; but we're sorry, there's no chance of us publishing it: it's true that it's an unusual as well as difficult read, but the money-men are looming over our shoulders like vultures. In the great battlefield of literary as well as biological survival, what is required is replication—the environment rules in the matter of the survival of what-fits-in. Amazing oddities, unfortunately, are naturally snuffed out.

One can try saying—But evolution, as opposed to the moribundity of dinosaurs, in fact depends on the survival of the rogue-that-does-not-quite-fit-in. Its difficulty is to find a ground that through difficult times will nurture it. In the natural run of things, yes, most of such oddities will get snuffed out. But some may have a chance of staying the course as the environment changes and so becoming accepted—through the pages of *The Review*, of *The Press*; perhaps of *Bridge*?

CAREER MOVES

Jerome Klinkowitz

Neither would qualify as a good bet: Jack O'Brien passing up chances for an influential academic career, Gil Sorrentino swearing off self-promotion in the literary world, as the two of them came together in Spring, 1981, for the Gilbert Sorrentino Number that initiated *The Review of Contemporary Fiction*. Yet there's an inevitability to their conjunction twenty years ago, a necessity based on a shared opinion that in both of their cases conventional measures of success wouldn't add up. Plus a more evident conjunction of necessities now, for twenty years later each has become an ikon for independent success: Jack as the publisher of the Dalkey Archive Press, regarded even by writers far from its fold as the only sound publisher of serious fiction in America today, Gil as the sole survivor of innovative fiction's spectacular boom and bust.

I have to speak personally, because I knew each of them well before all this began; the Cisco Kid and Pancho, they were friends of mine. More than thirty years ago, Jack showed up in my office at Northern Illinois University, acknowledging that I was the only assistant professor with an armful of publications and announcing that he wanted to be the only graduate student with same. Would I show him how to do it? Of course: "my first student," even though he was less than two years younger than myself. I left DeKalb in 1972, for the associate professorship such publications would buy a twenty-eight-year-old. Jack hung on to write a doctoral dissertation for Jim Mellard, but all through the 1970s and into the 80s, we stayed in close touch, including a trip (in December, 1972) to New York, where we spent an evening with Sorrentino.

Gil was one of Jack's finds, part of his program to build up such a stack of publications that he could fly out of NIU with credentials so much stronger than just a doctorate from this institution would imply. In terms of careerism, the focus was on African-American fictionists; by letter, phone, and travel, my former student had covered the country interviewing figures both established and new (including the first serious look at an English teacher down at Jackson State named Alice Walker) and by 1973, two years ahead of my own first book-length study, published the seminal *Interviews with Black Writers*, of whom I was a dedicatee. Liveright, just ending its period under the directorship of the stately Gilbert Harrison, brought it out in both cloth and paperback. But Jack's true love had become Sorrentino and his habitat, the world of Brooklyn in the 1950s with young guys on G.I. Bill benefits fashioning a new world of literary modernism, one quite apart from the cosmology espoused by universities. Like Jack, Gil had hung out with new black writers, most notably LeRoi Jones. And as Jack would do, Gil had published a literary magazine, *Neon*, cranking it out in the most humble circumstances imaginable, from a mimeograph machine atop the kitchen table. But not as homely a situation as the birthplace for *The Review*, which in its genesis shared an address with Jack's mother.

Committing himself to the magazine was Jack's first derailment from the career track his professors at Northern Illinois University hoped he would pursue. Although the job market had collapsed, NIU still had hopes for its doctoral program, and putting Jack out there as a famous graduate, teaching at a major university and sending back students to the old mill, was an ideal—never to be realized, because despite his attractability, he refused anything but a local job at Illinois Benedictine College in nearby Lisle, Illinois, a short commute from Elmwood Park and his preparations for *The Review*. Plus the guy simply couldn't leave Chicago; on occasions when I'd come in from Cedar Falls, he'd show me all the classic places from the Berghoff Restaurant on West Adams and Gino's Pizzeria on East Superior to (so help me God) the naugahyde bar atop the John Hancock Building, three postmodern staples of the City of the Big Shoulders. He could crack up a table with his impression of Mayor Daley, but with the same insider's knowledge and grudging appreciation as shown by that other typical Chicagoan of the era, Mike Royko. It strikes me now that this was probably what Sorrentino, a generation before, had been doing with incomers like Fielding Dawson at the time when Gil had made the move from Brooklyn to the Village and could never imagine living anywhere else.

As for Gil, Jack's introduction got me into his work and into a correspondence that lasted into the 1990s, though the man spent almost all his time resisting what I'd wanted to do with him. Our letters are among Sorrentino's papers collected at the University of Delaware, and record the enthusiasms of a critic advocating the innovative fiction that enjoyed a brief popularity from the mid-1960s to the mid-1970s and the disclaimers, warnings, and attempts at tutelage by a figure who'd been there before that and who had no doubts he'd outlive the phenomenon. Looking back at the 1981 Sorrentino issue of *The Review*, it's evident why the man didn't want to be included in the Vonnegut-Brautigan-Barthelme-Sukenick-Federman progression, even as a precursor; his own roots were in another style of alternative line, the Whitman-Williams-Olson tradition that the universities, with their fixation on T.S. Eliot, had downgraded. Did this make him not much of a fictionist at all, just a poor man's Robert Creeley, as some were describing him when Jack came across his almost totally unnoticed fiction? Well, that was better than being shown off as the Cannonball Adderly of some disco-flavored, watered-down jazz. But Gil did accept job tips, especially those for better gigs than the one he had teaching part-time at a state college in New Jersey, a less-than-easy commute from West Street in the Village. And so after some conference appearances and a stellar visiting professorship at the University of Scranton, he wound up holding the Wallace Stegner Chair at Stanford. Read the Stegner biographies to learn about the hassle all that caused. Cisco drank the whiskey, Pancho drank the wine.

So here we have them: Gil just retired from a couple decades of financial and climatic bliss in the citrus groves of academe, while Jack sits atop his publishing empire at Illinois State University, the choice of Chicago high school graduates who don't want to be as close as DeKalb or as far away as Carbondale, and who aren't in the Big Ten swim of things. Each of them is the best in the business and has exactly what he wants, different as those desires are from typical careerist mainstreamers. The paths each followed are clear from "that 1981 *The Review* issue," idiosyncratic even now and completely off the wall in terms of what scholarship amounted to twenty years ago.

Scholarly magazines are generally open—open to whatever comes in on whichever writer, submissions that are refereed by a panel of disinterested outside experts. Some, like *Modern Fiction Studies*, alternate with special issues on individual authors or topics; others, like *Critique*, do them rarely; most, like *Contemporary Literature*, never deviate from the open format. *The Review* not only began with a single-author issue, but announced its program with an actual spreadsheet charting out the next four years in their entirety devoted to authors identified either singly or in pairs. Big names: John Hawkes, William S. Burroughs, Jack Kerouac, Julio Cortázar. Soon the net would be cast wider, but always for major figures: Carlos Fuentes, Italo Calvino, Michel Butor. Would Beckett and Borges be far behind? But mixed in were personal favorites: Paul Metcalf, Hubert Selby, Nicholas Mosley, Coleman Dowell, Aidan Higgins. The pattern was clear: here were European or Eurocentric North and South American writers continuing the tradition of obscurantist High Modernism. No Brautigans, no Vonneguts, no Sukenicks, no Katzes or Federmans. For a long time, no women, and just one African American (Ishmael Reed, with an emphasis on his Egyptology). Unlike *MFS*, *Crit*, and *ConLit*, this newly launched *Review* gave, despite its name, little sense of the "contemporary," if *contemporary* meant the 1980s. Its featured subjects were writers of the 1950s, their careers having taken direction before the great cultural turmoil of the American 1960s. Instead, the program spoke for a disaffinity with everything since those middle 1960s, from innovative fiction and feminism to multiculturalism and a skeptical view of literary canons. And at the head of it all was a writer whose opinions, voiced so brilliantly in letters to Jack and myself, informed (if not inspired) this editorial policy: Gilbert Sorrentino.

As for the inaugural issue itself, it is almost a personal statement. Fully one-quarter is Sorrentino himself: being interviewed by Jack O'Brien, opining on the act of creation, presenting part of a work-in-progress, and being remembered, in person and in print, by Hubert Selby and Toby Olson. Next come some conventional essays by acknowledged scholars, but then more personal responses, all written in the first person—no other critical journal, no other review of contemporary fiction, had ever asked its typesetter to hit the "I" key so often. Oddly enough, the most traditional piece comes from way out of left field: a freshly translated essay on *Tristram Shandy* from Viktor Shklovsky's *Theory of Prose*, a work first published (in Russian) in 1925.

What's Shklovsky's essay doing here? *Tristram Shandy* might relate to Sorrentino's *Mulligan Stew*, just as does Flann O'Brien's *At Swim-Two-Birds*, something Jack's own essay in this issue explains. But why Russian Formalism, something an editorial footnote announces will be a staple of future *Review*'s as well, apparently regardless of the individual focus?

The answer comes from what Jack was picking up from Gil all these years and working through in his own literary criticism—unpublished, but ever in progress. Gil's position is made clear in *Something Said*, the collection of a lifetime's essays the Dalkey Archive has brought back into print in an edition updated to 2001. A theme in Sorrentino's commentary is how aesthetic motives explain literary structure—for better (as in Hubert Selby's fiction) or for worse (as in John O'Hara's). For Gil, the cardinal sin is to use a device as an end in itself, letting writers slip out of their responsibilities to their materials so that they could more easily tell readers what they already know (for readers know the conventional devices as well as writers do). The best work, it stands to reason, is one in which the author makes no such escapes—a work that remains so self-enclosed that it can do its work without any need to explain itself in extraneous terms. Selby writes that way, we learn; and so, Jack O'Brien implies by printing Shklovsky's essay on a similar work here, does Sorrentino, for the Russian Formalist's appreciation of Sterne is voiced in the same terms that Gil uses in his interview and essay, that Jack employs in his critical piece, and that so many of the hand-picked contributors rely upon in their personal responses. As Shklovsky said, a work of art is best perceived against the background of (if not by way of association with) other works of art. The novels Gil himself writes, do; those works he dislikes, don't.

And so *The Review* began its run with a celebration of what other critics in other places were calling "metafiction." And as the metafictive impulse took hold, others who met the Russian Formalist test would be admitted to the fold, including Pynchon, Coover, and Barth. In terms of currency, metafiction was certainly out and about. But so were so many other things—culturally, much more important things—that the journal turned its back on, perhaps because they did not conform to this Formalist ideal.

Looking back on the period from almost a generation later, I can see a proscriptive rather than descriptive bent to Gil's work (which for a creative writer is fine) and to Jack's (a dubious trait for a critic and a contradiction for a scholar). For both guys, it has bred a sternness, an old-fashioned style of schoolmarmishness that's awkwardly out of character with the age. But then looking back to the absolutism of Shklovsky rather than to the relativism of Saussure might be the best way to start correcting the nature of an era one deplores.

In contrasting the nature of Jack and Gil's in-crowd with their outs, it seems none of the insiders is very happy. Has anyone ever seen O'Brien or Sorrentino smile? The guy who came to my office door thirty years ago was scowling; so was the man he took me to meet on West Street in the Village a couple years later. Surveying the whole extended crowd, there seems to be so much unhappiness: Hawkes in his terrible fragility, Pynchon hiding in paranoia, Coover (if we are to believe what he told Richard Elman) trying to climb out from under the CIA—and, most characteristically, Barth, that ultimate university careerist who, having studied at Johns Hopkins and Julliard and served his mean apprenticeship, got piped on board just as the ship was seized by pirates and turned from sailing the high seas of purist Modernism to a series of dirty skirmishes and coastal raids. How different from the mood in which others have lived their lives. How different from the wry but gentle humor of Vonnegut, the exuberance of Sukenick, the artful play of Paley and Katz, the expressiveness of Major, the flamboyant joy of Federman. How different from me.

But no one takes either route without friends. How I ever got mixed up with Jack and Gil in the first place must perplex them. Yet there are still writers out there on whom we agree: Kenneth Gangemi, for example. Michael Stephens. Each of whom I have heard laugh. So maybe it's not such a hard life after all. Ay, Cisco? Ay, Pancho!

SORRENTINO'S OPUS

Toby Olson

In a 1981 article called "Sorrentino's Past," I set out to argue that the old-time confusion between the author's fictions and his autobiography and "character" were again in error, or at least produced unfruitful conclusions when it came to Gilbert Sorrentino's writings. We all knew of the tight, exclusionary structures of these novels, their artifice, and Sorrentino had been explicit, pointedly in reference to characters in the supposed *roman à clef* of *Imaginative Qualities of Actual Things* (in a *Vort* #6 interview with Barry Alpert) when he spoke of Leo Kaufman: "The model for Leo Kaufman: how do I know if that man is washed up? I mean he's liable to have another 50 years of creative life, you know. He may become a Yeats in old age, or a Thomas Hardy. I don't know. But *my* Leo Kaufman is forever fixed, you see, in prose. He's a fictitious character who's nailed down in that book" (25). Not so firmly nailed down, however, since he appears again later, in *Odd Number* and *Rose Theatre*, for example, and one might wonder where he was and what he was doing between these books, which is fancy, but part of the experience of reading Sorrentino's novels nonetheless, not one book of course, but the entire opus, and that over time. Here's the opening paragraph from a most recent Sorrentino fiction, "*Life and Letters*," which appeared in *Conjunctions* 37:

> Some three or four years ago, Edward Krefitz published a story that, as is the case with many stories, contained elements of his past life, elements, of course, disguised, twisted, corrupted, embellished, romanticized, and wholly fanciful. A few people recognized themselves as models for characters in the story, and were, predictably, chagrined or flattered, depending on the quality of the fiction's distortion of their being. They all wished, surely, to be *accurately portrayed*, certainly; but there is accuracy and then there is meanspiritedness. So they muttered. (427)

How not to see this passage in relation to *Imaginative Qualities* and the issue it raises; how not see the literary life of the city in the story that follows in relation to the one depicted in that book published more than thirty years ago? And why not see them this way, both as analogue and a kind of fulfillment of the terms of that earlier novel? Here the writer receives his just dues, his characters become their models and rise up to sting him, in comedy of course, less bitter now, a friendlier irony.

The city has changed, or the prose has. The touch is lighter, the humor less sly, strangely celebratory now? If there was space between the structure of sentences and wit, that's been overcome. Have characters from that early novel changed their names, become more mature as they are reworked by the author, discovered, after absence, by the reader? Has the author changed, matured, developed, grown older? Or had the writer of an essay such as this become less concerned with precision than nuance?

I'm looking at the cover of the first *Review of Contemporary Fiction*, the Gilbert Sorrentino Number, and there he is, sitting in a chair, with a beard, writing longhand on a clipboard in a drawing made by Christopher Sorrentino, his son, and I can't believe the skill. Then I remember, Oh, yes, Chris must have been in his early twenties at the time, not the child of five or six that I had met in the mid-1960s in Aspen, Colorado. I remember a hike into the mountains, Gil, Jonathan Williams, maybe Ron Johnson, sitting naked in a hot spring, none of us yet of a certain age. There are those who romance the past. I am one of them, and even Leo Kaufman might have been there, somewhere. The drawing is of Chris seeing his father, making an appearance, appearing for me once again, not unlike Leo Kaufman appears after absence, and who is to say whether his eyes are his baby eyes or not?

It is hard to separate the artist from his work when one knows the artist, and in the case of Sorrentino, it is hard to isolate the individual work for meaningful consideration, once you have read the entire opus, even if you don't know him. His city has changed through the years, as has its analogue in these novels' prose, but it is recognizable even as it sits waiting for animation between the books. This seems true, too, of his characters. There somewhere, even Lorna Flambeaux is, waiting to reappear in *Rose Theatre*, throbbing like the dreaded kohlrabi of *Red The Fiend*, which takes its place once again as well, in passing, in *Gold Fools*.

There seems two things to be said. With many great writers (Faulkner, Melville, James) the structural integrity of individual books is finally an insignificant matter. You can throw away passages and characters, you can readjust narrative order, and still have the books. It's the prose that matters, the way sentences create characters and the world they live in. Flann O'Brien knew this and treated it comically in *At-Swim-Two-Birds*, and it's significant that Sorrentino took it from O'Brien, then extended the idea of it, for *Mulligan Stew*: just a few characters (people?) recycled again and again throughout literary history, each transformed and "nailed down" when the artist who takes them on has the skill for it.

And the second thing, so reasonable in the case of Sorrentino and the reappearance of his characters and places, is that it's the entire opus that must finally draw us beyond the individual books. His is a long story, people come and go, then come again, like real people rediscovered over the years. This is why his writing is so lifelike, as life goes on.

WORKS BY GILBERT SORRENTINO

Fiction

The Sky Changes. New York: Hill and Wang, 1966. San Francisco: North Point Press, 1986. Normal: Dalkey Archive Press, 1998.
Steelwork. New York: New York: Pantheon Books, 1970. Elmwood Park: Dalkey Archive Press, 1992.
Imaginative Qualities of Actual Things. New York: Pantheon Books, 1971. Normal: Dalkey Archive Press, 1991. Rpt. 1995.
Splendide-Hôtel. New York: New Directions, 1973. Elmwood Park: Dalkey Archive Press, 1984.
Flawless Play Restored: The Masque of Fungo. Los Angeles: Black Sparrow Press, 1974.
Mulligan Stew. New York: Grove, 1979. Rpt. 1987. Normal: Dalkey Archive Press, 1996.
Aberration of Starlight. New York: Random House, 1980. Rpt. 1981. Normal: Dalkey Archive Press, 1993.
Crystal Vision. San Francisco: North Point Press, 1981. Harmondsworth: Penguin, 1982.
Blue Pastoral. San Francisco: North Point Press, 1983.
Odd Number. San Francisco: North Point Press, 1985.
A Beehive Arranged On Humane Principles. New York: Grenfell Press, 1986.
Rose Theatre. Elmwood Park: Dalkey Archive Press, 1987.
Misterioso. Elmwood Park: Dalkey Archive Press, 1989.
Under The Shadow. Elmwood Park: Dalkey Archive Press, 1993.
Red The Fiend. New York: Fromm, 1995.
Pack of Lies. Normal: Dalkey Archive Press, 1997.
Gold Fools. Los Angeles: Green Integer, 2001.
Little Casino. Minneapolis: Coffee House, 2002.

Poetry

The Darkness Surrounds Us. Highlands: Jonathan Williams Publisher, 1960.
Black and White. New York: Totem Press, 1964.
The Perfect Fiction. New York: Norton, 1968.
Corrosive Sublimate. Los Angeles: Black Sparrow, 1971.
A Dozen Oranges. Los Angeles: Black Sparrow, 1976.
Sulpiciæ Elegidia: Elegiacs of Sulpicia. Mt. Horeb: Perishable Press, 1977.
White Sail. Santa Barbara: Black Sparrow, 1977.
The Orangery. Austin: University of Texas Press, 1978. Los Angeles: Sun & Moon, 1995.
Selected Poems: 1958-1980. Santa Barbara: Black Sparrow, 1981.

Criticism

Something Said: Essays by Gilbert Sorrentino. San Francisco: North Point Press, 1984. Normal: Dalkey Archive Press, 2001.

Ever The Consummate, Intransigent Modernist

David Andrews

A Review of the Updated Edition of *Something Said: Essays by Gilbert Sorrentino* (The Dalkey Archive Press, 20001. 364 pp. $14.95)

When first published by North Point in 1984, Gilbert Sorrentino's *Something Said* was a wonderful collection of essays, one of those supreme yet secret works with the potential to transform readers interested in innovative art and literature. Joyously, the book is not only still wonderful, it is even more so. This accomplishment is the glad result of the fact that Mr. Sorrentino, over the course of a long, unswerving career, has never *once* changed, for the premises and values espoused in the last essays of the updated *Something Said* are identical to those espoused in the initial essays of the inaugural edition. Though he has deepened and complicated his ideas while varying and enlarging his critical focus, Mr. Sorrentino has not given an inch when it comes to his twin ideological obsessions: an aesthete, he still believes in the autonomy of the aesthetic, and he is still obsessed with assessing aesthetic value.

That is to say, the updated edition of *Something Said* reconfirms the notion that its author is at once a *consummate* and an *intransigent* modernist. Mr. Sorrentino's criticism verifies what his art suggests, that his classically modernist belief in the autonomy of artwork and artist necessitates a belief in the uselessness, culturally speaking, of both. His unstinting belief in artistic uselessness has other critical corollaries, too, e.g., his abiding belief in the anti-referential function of art, which means art is and always has been objective, thingly, autotelic, an end in itself rather than a tool, a communiqué, a datum. From the "Preface" of the first edition to "Writing and Writers: *Disjecta Membra*," the last piece of the updated edition, this nonutilitarian insistence remains constant; even the title, an allusion to Maurice Blanchot, extends this point. Further, this idea apparently necessitates the increasing antiessentialism of Mr. Sorrentino's ouevre, which on first glance seems to insist on the meaninglessness of word and world so as to conform with prevailing postmodernist ideas, i.e., with Continental and Pragmatist dismantlings of "fact" and "value." Not so—indeed, not even secondarily. The author's anti-referential antiessentialism is instead a way of supporting the all-important modernist notion of aesthetic autonomy, which is necessary to any *essentialist* defense of intrinsic value. Ironically, only if the supreme artwork, like the supreme artist, is viewed as independent and isolate, beyond contingency and circumstance, can that artwork, like that artist, be justified as "supreme," "best," or even, for that matter, "better."

Still, for the uninitiated, this defense of autonomy may not be the book's most immediately impressive component. That distinction is likely to go to the acerbic energy, not to mention the astonishing eloquence, of Mr. Sorrentino's opinions, especially those that manifest as hierarchical evaluations of aesthetic merit. Of Mr. Sorrentino, Robert Creeley has said that the "necessity to make judgement, to define value, is *always* primary in this writer, no matter the formal means employed or the technical pattern." In tandem with fictional works like *Imaginative Qualities of Actual Things* (1971) and *Splendide-Hôtel* (1973), *Something Said* validates Creeley's point. One difference between the original and supplemental portions of *Something Said* is that the latter are not nearly as relentless as the former. The North Point edition is characterized not only by its affectionate and perceptive treatments of William Carlos Williams, Louis Zukofsky, Jack Spicer, Edward Dahlberg, Paul Blackburn, and William Bronk but by its tomahawkings of Marianne Moore, John Updike, and John Gardner as well. While there are plenty of implacable opinions in the supplemental portion, there are no extended denunciations. It is unclear whether this is a result of Mr. Sorrentino's "softening" over time or of changes in his situation as a critic. Regardless, it is clear that the same heated modernism that impelled the aforementioned denunciations still impels his criticism.

And again, it is hard to neglect Mr. Sorrentino's gift for the exact and exacting statement. Who else but Mr. Sorrentino would, in an essay on Nathanael West's *Day of the Locust*, have characterized bestseller lists so unforgettably as "[a]reas of idiocy within which various degrees of the spurious are compared"? Who else, in praising Bronk's poetry, would argue that, to "understand that the world is not ours for the taking, and to understand further that it will not yield up anything that it does not intrinsically possess, seems to me to be the only program that a serious writer can suscribe to"? Or again, of Williams's Stecher trilogy: "The novel is an invention, something that is made; it is not the expression of 'self'; it does not mirror reality. If it is any good at all it mirrors the processes of the real, but, being selective, makes a form that allows us to see these processes with clarity." As Mr. Sorrentino says anent Zukofsky, essays such as this "cannot be licked off the page." They are perfections, hence in Mr. Sorrentino's economy, they are nonutilitarian objects. In his "Preface" to the first edition, he notes that the purpose of criticism is to be useful, transitive; still, he says, the best criticism "begins, oddly, to detach itself from its cause, and to float free of it. It begins to move, that is, toward the literature that it purports to be 'talking about.' It is as if it *wants to be* literature too, as if it cannot countenance its function as that of the useful but wishes to approach the condition of the useless." Mr. Sorrentino's own criticism, advertently or no, fulfills this scenario. Though his essays are accurate and incisive, by his own terminology they are beyond "mere" accuracy. They are, to be succinct, art.

The above quotations are from the original *Something Said.* The new sections are no less eloquent. And no less comic: witness the extended "sacred cow" metaphor in Mr. Sorrentino's 1985 review of Calvino's *Mr. Palomar.* This spirited catachresis (which is far longer, incidentally, than the quote that follows) praises Calvino's decision to scuttle "characterization, conflict, linear development, and closure," four tropes Mr. Sorrentino considers "the flesh and blood of the sacred cow of conventional fiction, which, though dead for more than a century, has been reappearing, without surcease, as the weird monstrosity whose post-mortem twitches are mistaken for life." Mr. Sorrentino is not an entertainer, but his work is entertaining, and that may be the crux of his modernist rhetoric, which so consistently and persuasively insists on innovation.

One way in which the new sections do supersede the old involves the types of essays included. There are, proportionally, more non-review essays in the new section than in the old. Indeed, almost all of Mr. Sorrentino's oldest essays are reviews, including those from the days when he wrote for *Kulchur* and a variety of little magazines. (I imagine several of those essays in much the way Mr. Sorrentino imagines Koufax's remarkable pitches in bush-league contexts. One of his analytic yet visionary reviews must have seemed aberrant, not to mention overpowering, in the more obscure little magazines: *Christ, here it comes.*) Still, some of the strongest and longest essays in the first edition are not reviews. For example, "The Act of Creation and Its Artifact," a classic essay whose ideas of creation reflect those of Baudelaire, Rimbaud, Williams, and Blanchot, is one of the few non-review pieces in the original; "Black Mountaineering" and "Genetic Coding" are two more. Yet even the reviews tend away from the glib, commercial function of the standard review, and several even idealize the "independent" essay, for example, the pieces on Williams, Zukofsky, Spicer, Dahlberg, and Blackburn. The new edition includes a greater number of non-review pieces, essays that realize the brilliance hinted at by the early reviews and demonstrated by the various independent critical pieces. These include essays and lectures that have appeared in forums such as *Conjunctions*, *The Review of Contemporary Fiction*, *Context*, and so on. In these works, Mr. Sorrentino's critical intelligence quickly detaches from its divers objects so as to float more freely in a space merging artistic and critical mastery.

Though there are many more things I could say, I will close by glossing an idea mentioned earlier. *Something Said* has considerable transformative power. When I first read the book eight years ago, I shared Randall Jarrell's wrongheaded view of Williams as poetry's Grandma Moses, a view Mr. Sorrentino irascibly takes to pieces. Likewise, I had never read many of the poets and novelists I now revere, among them Zukofsky, Spicer, Bronk, Blackburn, Dahlberg, Creeley, Lorine Niedecker, Flann O'Brien, David Markson, Coleman Dowell, Charles Olson, John Hawkes, and others. Mr. Sorrentino, through passion and crystalline prose, convinced me to read all of these writers—which is to say *Something Said* is, as the narrator of *Imaginative Qualities* calls his own novel, an antidote to ignorance. This is especially true for younger audiences, who otherwise might never encounter a remarkable but relatively obscure poet like Bronk. *Something Said* is, then, a distinguished addition to American modernist aesthetics, as well as a delightful critical work whose taste-making is trustworthy, spirited, and durable.

Notes Section: Contributors

David Andrews teaches American literature and writing at the University of Illinois at Chicago. His essays have appeared in a number of collections and journals, including *The Review of Contemporary Fiction*, *The Chicago Review*, *Film Criticism*, *Nabokov Studies*, *Leviathan*, *Context*, etc. His book, *Aestheticism, Nabokov, and Lolita* (Edwin Mellen), appeared in 1999. Currently, Andrews is an associate editor at *Bridge*. ♦ **Kevin Blasko** is a writer living in Chicago whose work has previously appeared in *The New Art Examiner*. He can be reached at kevin_blasko@hotmail.com. ♦ **B.C. Brown** edited *The History of Panty Hose in America* (1999 Espresso Press) and used to be a card dealer. Now she lives in Minnesota. ♦ **William Cordova** is an artist from Miami, represented by NFA Space in Chicago and Ambrosino Gallery in Miami. ♦ **Brian Costello** hosts *The Brian Costello Show with Brian Costello*, a live talk-show held every other month at Quimby's Bookstore in Chicago. His stories have appeared in *the2ndhand* and *Sleepwalk*. ♦ **Joel Craig** is a poet and DJ. He lives in Chicago and coordinates The Danny's Reading Series. ♦ **Elizabeth Crane's** work has been featured in publications including *The Sycamore Review*, *Washington Square*, *Weep*, *New York Stories*, *Book Magazine*, and *The Chicago Reader*. Her story collection will be published by Little, Brown in 2003. A New York City native, she now lives in Chicago. ♦ **Caitlin O'Connor Creevy** grew up in Mississippi and Chicago. She became a columnist for the *Chicago Tribune* at age seventeen, before attending New York University. Her work has appeared in numerous publications, including *Open City*; *word.com*; *Personals* [a Houghton Mifflin anthology], and many others. She is now attending USC Graduate School. ♦ **Jeanne Dunning's** work has internationally recognized since the mid-1980s and it has been included in many notable exhibitions such as the Whitney Biennial, the Venice Biennale, the Sydney Biennale, and *New Photography 14* at MOMA. She has had one person shows at The

Hirshhorn Museum in Washington D.C., The Museum of Contemporary Art in Chicago, Magazin 4 Voralberger Kunstverien in Bregenz, Austria, and the Konstmuseet in Malm, Sweden. The Berkeley Art Museum is organizing a traveling survey of her work which will open in 2004. She is currently the department chairperson of Art Theory and Practice at Northwestern University. ♦ **Jan Estep** is an artist and editor at *New Art Examiner*. She's interested in language, theories of knowledge, and the cultural mediation of nature. ♦ **Howard Fonda**, an artist, independant curator and general ignoramus, is very excited to be contributing to *Bridge*. He would like to thank his mother, his father, his girlfriend and Henry David Thoreau. Fonda resides in Chicago. ♦ **Michelle Grabner and Brad Killam** run The Suburban, an exhibition space in Oak Park, Illinois ♦ **Ryan Kenealy** enjoys tipping vending machines more for the element of danger inherent than the free cola. His story *Yellow and Maroon* appeared in *Open City* #7. ♦ **Jerome Klinkowitz** has for many years served as professor of English and University Distinguished Scholar at the University of Northern Iowa. He is the author of forty books, including novels, collections of short stories, and studies of literature, philosophy, art, music, sport, and air combat narratives; his latest book, *You've Got To Be Carefully Taught* (Southern Illinois), was released in 2001. In addition, since 1979, Klinkowitz has served as editor of the contemporary American literature section of *American Literary Scholarship*. ♦ **Meredith Goldsmith** is an artist and writer who lives and works in Chicago. ♦ **Michael Jefferson** graduated from the University of Michigan in 1995. His work has appeared in *New Art Examiner* and he has exhibited at Cliff Dwellers. He can be reached at jeffersonjefferson@hotmail.com. ♦ **Shana Lutker** is an artist living in Chicago. ♦ **Robert McLaughlin** is the senior editor of *The Review of Contemporary Fiction*. The author of many scholarly works on contemporary literature, including a long essay on Mary Caponegro that appeared in the Fall 2001 issue of *The Review*, McLaughlin currently serves as an assistant professor in the English Department at Illinois State University. ♦ **Joyelle McSweeney's** first book, *The Red Bird*, was selected by Allen Grossman for the *Fence* Modern Poets Series and is available from FenceBooks. ♦ **Joe Meno** is a full-time professor of fiction writing at Columbia College Chicago. His new book is *How the Hula Girl Sings*, out by Harper Collins. There was a month in his recent life where he was convinced ghosts were trying to communicate with him through what strangers would say to him on the train. ♦ **CJ Mitchell** was born in Stornoway, Scotland, and moved to Chicago in 1998. He has been involved with occasional writing projects since the mid-80s, and recently started the CD label False Walls: www.falsewalls.com. CJ works administratively with Goat Island Performance Group (with whom he also collaborates on writing projects) and at Performing Arts Chicago. *Walking in Chicago* was originally written for Matthew Goulish's class "Systems of Writing" at SAIC. ♦ **Gean Moreno** is an artist and writer from Miami, represented by NFA Space in Chicago. His writing has appeared in *New Art Examiner* and he has also exhibited at Kevin Bruk Gallery in in Miami. ♦ **Nicholas Mosley** is the distinguished author of more than twenty books of fiction and nonfiction. He is especially well known for his innovative novels, including *Impossible Object*, *Catastrophe Practice*, and *Hopeful Monsters*, which won the Whitbread Award in 1991. Currently, Mosley lives and works in London. ♦ **Iain Muirhead** is an artist and curator living in Chicago. Muirhead founded NFA SPACE in 1996 with fellow artist and curator Amavong Panya to introduce challenging contemporary art in all media by emerging artists within a curatorially driven exhibition context. Three artists from the NFA SPACE 2001 program were selected for the 2002 Whitney Bienniel. Iain spends his evenings painting and learning to fly. ♦ **Toby Olson** has written many innovative novels, including *Seaview* (which won the PEN/Faulkner Award), *The Life of Jesus*, and most recently, *Write Letter to Billy* (Coffee House). Olson has also written more than twenty books of poetry. His work has appeared in over two hundred newspapers, magazines, and anthologies. Now retired from his teaching position at Temple, Olson divides his time between Philadelphia and North Truro, Massachusetts. ♦ **D.A. Powell** is the author of *Tea* (Wesleyan, 1998) and *Lunch* (Wesleyan, 2000). He was appointed Briggs-Copeland Lecturer in Poetry at Harvard University in the Fall of 2001. ♦ **Peter Richards** was born in Urbana, Illinois in 1967. He teaches at Tufts University and lives in Somerville, Massachusetts. His first book, *Oubliette*, was released in 2001 by Verse Press. ♦ **Amavong Panya** is an artist and curator living in Chicago. Panya founded NFA SPACE in 1996 with fellow artist and curator Iain Muirhead to introduce challenging contemporary art in all media by emerging artists within a curatorially driven exhibition context. Three artists from the NFA SPACE 2001 program were selected for the 2002 Whitney Bienniel. Amavong spends late nights drawing stars and polishing his motorcycle. ♦ **Greg Purcell** will be entering therapy on Tuesday. ♦ **Kevin Sampsell** lives and works in Portland, Oregon. He is the author of a few small books. He has recently had written works published in *Rain Taxi*, *Weep*, *3rd Bed*, *Cimmaron Review*, *2 girls review*, and *Little Engines*. ♦ **Alex Shakar** is the author of the novel *The Savage Girl* and short story collection *City in Love*. He currently lives in Chicago. ♦ **Harvey Strub** writes and mails a letter to the President every Monday. His letters have appeared in *Pindeldyboz* and *Salt Hill*. ♦ Dan Raeburn lives in Chicago, where he spends a lot of time reading comic books and writing about them in his irregularly self-published magazine, *The Imp*. ♦ **Ralph Syverson** draws like a butterfly and paints like a bee. ♦ **M.D. Tschaepe** is currently doing phenomenological and psycho-analytic research on the significance of first names, as well as addressing the question, "What is the father?". ♦ There is nothing painter **Patrick W. Welch** would rather do than languish in miserable obscurity and wallow in failure, but his gallery Lyons Wier seems to have other plans for him. Look for forthcoming exhibits of his infamous "hate" paintings in Chicago. Meanwhile Welch continues to get really fat, as well as old. ♦ **Curtis White's** most recent novel is *Requiem*. His next novel, *America's Magic Mountain*, will appear in 2003. He also edits *Context, a Forum for Literary Arts and Culture*.

THE FIRST EVER *BRIDGE* SURVEY

Please fill out the following survey and help us sell you to our advertisers. It"ll keep Bridge organized and stable and maybe even lucid when it needs it.

How does it feel to be wanted? Be honest. You love it. You know you do.

1. Zip code:________________
2. Age: ☐ under 24 ☐ 25-39 ☐ 40-54 ☐ 55+
3. Sex: ☐ Female ☐ Male ☐ "Othered"
4. Are you a: ☐ home owner ☐ renter ☐ apartment/condo owner
5. How many live in your home: ☐ 1-2 ☐ 3-4 ☐ 4+
6. Total Yearly household income: ☐ under $25,000 ☐ $25,000-$50,000 ☐ $50,000-$100,000 ☐ $100,000-$150,000 ☐ over $150,000
7. Education: ☐ high school diploma or equivalent ☐ college ☐ graduate school ☐ post-graduate
8. Occupation: ☐ art professional ☐ education ☐ business ☐ law ☐ medicine ☐ student ☐ technology ☐ other________________
9. Do you subscribe to *Bridge*? ☐ yes ☐ no
10. I first heard about *Bridge* from: ☐ friend ☐ gift ☐ library ☐ bookstore ☐ school ☐ newstand ☐ other
11. After I read *Bridge*, I: ☐ save for reference ☐ share ☐ recycle ☐ other______________
12. How many other people read the magazine in addition to yourself? ☐ none ☐ 1-2 ☐ 3-4 ☐ 5+
13. My favorite sections are (check only two): ☐ Readings ☐ Culture & Critique ☐ Fiction ☐ Poetry ☐ Interviews ☐ Project Pages
14. I would like to read more about:

____
____
____
____

15. Have you visited our website? ☐ yes ☐ no If yes, how often? ☐ once a week ☐ once a month ☐ occasionally
16. On average, I go to galleries or museums: ☐ once a week or more ☐ 2-3 times a month ☐ once a month ☐ occasioanlly
17. I regularly purchase this many books a month ☐ 0-1 ☐2-4 ☐ 4-5 ☐ 6+
18. On average, I go to the movies: ☐ once a week or more ☐ 2-3 times a month ☐ once a month ☐ occasionally
19. I regularly purchase this many cds/tapes/records a month: ☐ 0-1 ☐ 2-4 ☐ 5-7 ☐ 8+
20. I shop for clothes/cosmetics this many times a year: ☐ 1-3 times ☐ 4-6 ☐ 6-10 ☐ once a month or more
21. Do you own a car? ☐ yes ☐ no If yes: ☐ compact ☐ family ☐ sedan ☐ sport ☐ luxury ☐ SUV
22. On average, I spend the following amount on art per year: ☐ $100-$500 ☐ $500-$1,000 ☐ $1,000-$5,000 ☐ $5,000-$10,000 ☐ $10,000+
23. Do you drink alcohol? ☐ yes ☐ no If yes, do you order alcohol by name? ☐ yes ☐ no Which do you prefer? ☐ beer ☐ wine ☐ spirits
24. Including breakfast and lunch, I dine out: ☐ everyday ☐ 3-4 times a week ☐ 1-2 times a week ☐ occasionally
25. I regularly purchase this many videotapes/DVDs a month: ☐ 0-1 ☐ 2-4 ☐ 5-7 ☐ 8+
26. Do you feel alone in the world?
27. Name three other magazines you read regularly:

a.____
b.____
c.____

28. Additional Comments:

____
____
____
____
____
____
____
____
____
____

Draw a picture of yourself here:

Visit our website
www.bridgemagazine.org

fold on dotted line

place stamp here

BRIDGE
1357 N. Ashland #3A
Chicago IL 60622

tape along this edge